Operational Poverty Targeting by Proxy Means Tests

DEVELOPMENT ECONOMICS AND POLICY

Series edited by Franz Heidhues, Joachim von Braun and Manfred Zeller

Vol. 67

PL ACADEMIC RESEARCH

Operational Poverty Targeting by Proxy Means Tests

Models and Policy Simulations for Malawi

S. Idriss Nazaire Houssou

PL ACADEMIC RESEARCH

Bibliographic Information published by the Deutsche Nationalbibliothek
The Deutsche Nationalbibliothek lists this publication in the Deutsche Nationalbibliografie; detailed bibliographic data is available in the internet at http://dnb.d-nb.de.

Published with financial support of DAAD - Deutscher Akademischer Austauschdienst and IFPRI - International Food Policy Research Institute, USA

Library of Congress Cataloging-in-Publication Data

Houssou, Nazaire, 1976- author.
Operational poverty targeting by proxy means tests : models and policy simulations for Malawi / S. Idriss Nazaire Houssou.
pages cm. — (Development economics and policy ; vol. 67)
„Published with financial support of DAAD - Deutscher Akademischer Austauschdienst and IFPRI - International Food Policy Research Institute, USA."
Originally presented as the author's thesis (doctoral)—University of Hohen heim, 2010.
Includes bibliographical references.
ISBN-13: 978-3-631-62570-5
ISBN-10: 3-631-62570-7
1. Poverty—Statistical methods. 2. Poverty—Malawi—Statistical methods. 3. Income—Malawi—Statistical methods. 4. Economic development projects—Malawi—Evaluation. 5. Economic development—Malawi—Statistical methods. 6. Economic development—Statistical methods. 7. Malawi—Economic policy. I. Title. II. Series: Development economics and policy ; Bd. 67.
HC79.P6H668 2013
339.460727—dc23

2013020343

ISSN 0948-1338
ISBN 978-3-631-62570-5

PL Academic Research is an imprint of Peter Lang GmbH.

Peter Lang – Frankfurt am Main · Bern · Bruxelles · New York · Oxford · Warszawa · Wien

www.peterlang.de

Editors' Foreword

The issue of targeting public policy has been a long standing challenge for policymakers and development practitioners. Many developing countries target a range of programs, such as subsidized agricultural inputs, credit and extension as well as basic health care, food aid, and other safety net measures to the poorer segments of the population. However, policymakers and development practitioners are confronted with the lack of operationally reliable methods for identifying the targeted population affected by poverty. As a result, most development programs are loosely targeted and therefore fail to reach their intended beneficiaries, the poor.

The research in this volume seeks to address the challenge of targeting. The author develops alternative proxy means test models that might improve the targeting efficiency of development programs. This book is based on three peer-reviewed articles which have been reprinted with the journals' permissions. The author also provides an introductory chapter which sets the scene along with a final chapter summarizing the major findings in the main articles and their policy implications.

Using the example of Malawi, the author uses a set of innovative statistical methods and econometric tools, including out-of-sample validation tests, receiver operating characteristic curves, and bootstrapped simulations to develop proxy indicator systems for targeting poor households in urban and rural areas of Malawi. Furthermore, the work demonstrates that using such alternative systems can be more target- and cost-efficient than the currently used methods for targeting development programs, such as the Farm Input Subsidy Program (FISP) formerly known as the Agricultural Input Support Program. More importantly, the methodology applied in this research can be extended to other developing countries which have recent nationally representative datasets containing household expenditures and proxy indicators of poverty, e.g. household demography, housing, clothing, education, assets, and occupation.

Achieving the Millennium Development Goals requires – among other policy measures- the effective targeting of the poorest, the vulnerable, and the population that has been left behind. Improvements to the mechanisms that target are essential in the process. We hope that this book will stimulate the academic and policy debate on how best to target the poor in the practice of development.

Prof. Dr. Joachim von Braun, Center for Development Research (ZEF), University of Bonn, Bonn, Germany.
Prof. Dr. Franz Heidhues, Institute of Agricultural Economics and Social Sciences in the Tropics and Subtropics, University of Hohenheim, Stuttgart, Germany.
Prof. Dr. Manfred Zeller, Institute of Agricultural Economics and Social Sciences in the Tropics and Subtropics, University of Hohenheim, Stuttgart, Germany.

Acknowledgments

I am deeply grateful to Prof. Zeller for his guidance and supervision during the course of this work. I would like to thank Prof. Piepho for his invaluable advices on the statistical analyses and his review of the papers included in this book. I would also like to express my profound gratitude to Prof. Heidhues for his extensive support. The publications on which this book is based had benefited from useful comments and suggestions from various anonymous reviewers and I wish to thank them all.

I would like to extend my deep gratitude to Ms. Contag, Mrs. Schumacher, and Ms. Mayer for extensive administrative assistance. I am grateful to my former colleagues and friends at the University of Hohenheim (Germany). I would like to express my warm appreciation to my former colleagues in the poverty assessment team: Gabriela, Julia, and Stefan at the University of Goettingen (Germany) and Anthony Leegwater at the IRIS Center (University of Maryland, USA) for fruitful exchanges. I also thank the surveyed households and the National Statistics Office of Malawi for generously providing the IHS2 dataset on which this work is based. Finally, I would like to express my profound gratitude to my family, especially my father and my mother for their love, support, and encouragements.

I highly appreciate the financial support of the German Exchange Academic Service (DAAD).

Nazaire S. Idriss Houssou
Washington D.C., March 2013

Table of Contents

List of Tables 13

Abbreviations and Acronyms 15

Chapter I 17
1. Introduction 17
  1.1 Background to the research 17
  1.2 Problem statement 19
  1.3 Research objectives and organization of the book 21
  1.4 Targeting in the literature 23
    1.4.1 The concept of poverty: Theoretical considerations 24
    1.4.2 Targeting the poor: Empirical methods 25
    1.4.3 Proxy means tests in the literature 29
References 35

Chapter II: Targeting the Poor and Smallholder Farmers: Empirical evidence from Malawi 39
1. Introduction 39
2. Data and methodology 41
  2.1 Data and theoretical framework 41
  2.2 Model estimation methods 42
    2.2.1 Variable selection 42
    2.2.2 Estimating the proxy means tests 42
  2.3 Accuracy measures and robustness tests 45
    2.3.1 Accuracy measures 45
    2.3.2 Assessing the predictive power of the models 46
3. Targeting accuracy of the proxy means tests: Empirical results 47
  3.1 Model predictive performances 47
  3.2 Targeting poverty using ROC curves: Examples from Malawi 49
  3.3 How sensitive are the models to the poverty line? 50
  3.4 Spatial distribution of targeting errors 52
4. Conclusions 53
References 53

Annexes 56
Annex 1. Malawi's poverty rates by region and poverty line 56
Annex 2. Results of the maximum likelihood estimates (rural model) 57
Annex 3. Malawi's rural poverty model calibrated to the national poverty line 58

Chapter III: Operational Models for Improving the Targeting Efficiency of Development Policies: A systematic comparison of different estimation methods using out-of-sample tests 59
1. Introduction 59
2. Data and estimation methods 61
2.1 Data 61
2.2 Model estimation methods 62
2.2.1 Poverty predictors and sample selections 62
2.2.2 Estimation methods 64
2.2.3 Predicting the household poverty status 68
2.3 Targeting ratios and robustness tests 70
2.3.1 Targeting ratios 70
2.3.2 Model validations 71
3. Results and discussions 73
3.1 Modelling the household poverty status: Empirical results 73
3.2 Aggregate performances of the estimation methods 77
3.3 Assessing model sensitivity to the poverty line 80
3.4 Comparing model targeting errors across welfare deciles 82
4. Concluding remarks 84
References 85
Annexes 88
Annex 1. Sample size by model type 88
Annex 2. Weighted Least Square estimates (rural model) 89
Annex 3. Weighted Logit estimates (rural model) 90
Annex 4. Weighted Least Square estimates (urban model) 91
Annex 5. Weighted Logit estimates (urban model) 92

Chapter IV: To Target or Not to Target: The costs, benefits, and impacts of indicator-based targeting 93
1. Introduction 93
2. Targeted development programs: The Malawian context 95
3. The principles of targeting: A theoretical perspective 97
4. Data and methodology 100
4.1 Data 100

4.2 Estimating the models 101
4.2.1 Estimation method 101
4.2.2 Out-of-sample tests 102
4.2.3 Measuring model targeting performances 103
4.3 Policy simulations 104
5. Empirical results 110
5.1 How well do the models identify the poor? 110
5.2 Targeting performances of development policies 111
5.3 Evaluating the cost-effectiveness and impacts of targeting the poor: Policy simulations 112
5.3.2 Cost-efficiency, benefits, and impacts of targeting 112
5.4 Cost efficiency of targeted agricultural input support programs versus the new system 115
6. Conclusions and policy implications 117
References 118
Annexes 121
Annex 1. Quantile regression results (rural model) 121
Annex 2. Quantile regression results (urban model) 122
Annex 3. Costs of targeting 123

Chapter V: General Conclusions 125

General Appendices 129
Appendix 1: Map of Malawi 129
Appendix 2. Sample size and number of potential indicators by model type and estimation method 130
Appendix 3. Descriptive statistics of variables used in the rural model (full sample) 131
Appendix 4. Descriptive statistics of variables used in the rural model (calibration sample) 132
Appendix 5. Descriptive statistics of variables used in the rural model (validation sample) 133
Appendix 6. Descriptive statistics of variables used in the urban model (full sample) 134
Appendix 7. Descriptive statistics of variables used in the urban model (calibration sample) 135
Appendix 8. Descriptive statistics of variables used in the urban model (validation sample) 136

List of Tables (Chapter I)

Table 1. Overview of poverty targeting methods 27
Table 2. Actual vs. predicted household poverty status 31
Table 3. Indicators of targeting performances 32
Table 4. Selected studies on proxy means tests 33

Abbreviations and Acronyms

AISP	Agricultural Input Subsidy Program
BEAM	Basic Education Assistance Module
COICOP	Classification of Individual Consumption According to Purpose
FAO	Food and Agriculture Organization
EGS	Employment Guarantee Scheme
FIVIMS	Food Insecurity and Vulnerability Mapping System
GAPVU	Gabinete de Apoio à População Vulnerável
GDP	Gross Domestic Product
GoM	Government of Malawi
HDI	Human Development Index
HIPCs	Heavily Indebted Poor Countries
HPI	Human Poverty Index
IFPRI	International Food Policy Research Institute
IHS1	First Malawi Integrated Household Survey
IHS2	Second Malawi Integrated Household Survey
INAS	National Institute for Social Welfare
JCE	Junior Certificate of Education
KCAL	Kilocalorie
KG	Kilogram
LPM	Linear Probability Model
LSMS	Living Standard Measurement Survey
MASAF	Malawi Social Action Fund
MDGs	Millennium Development Goals
MK	Malawi Kwacha
MPRS	Malawi Poverty Reduction Strategy
MSCE	Malawi School Certificate of Education
NGOs	Non-Governmental Organizations
NPK	Nitrogen Phosphorus and Potassium (Fertilizer)
NSO	National Statistics Office
OLS	Ordinary Least Square
PAM	Program Against Malnutrition
PMS	Poverty Monitoring System
PMT	Proxy Means Tests

PPP	Purchasing Power Parity
PPS	Probability Proportional to Size
PROGRESA	Programa de Educacion, Salud y Alimentacion
PSLC	Primary School Leaving Certificate
PSU	Primary Sampling Units
PWP	Public Work Program
SAS	Statistical Analysis System
SISBEN	Sistema de Identificación de Beneficiarios
SPI	Starter Pack Initiative
ROC	Receiver Operating Characteristic
TIP	Targeted Input Program
TLU	Tropical Livestock Unit
UN	United Nations
UNDP	United Nations Development Program
USAID	United States Agency for International Development
WL	Weighted Logit
WLS	Weighted Least Square

CHAPTER I

1. Introduction

1.1 Background to the research

Eradicating poverty is one of the major challenges facing the developing world and the international community. The plethoric number of National, International, Non-Governmental Organizations, and advocacy groups fighting poverty on all its dimensions around the world just indicates the extent of the challenge.

More than one billion of people in the developing world live in absolute poverty (UN, 2009). Three out of four people in developing countries live in rural areas and most of them depend directly or indirectly on agriculture for their livelihood (World Bank, 2008). While, the Asian and Latin American countries have made significant progress in reducing poverty in the past decades, the results have been rather mixed in sub-Saharan Africa and the poverty rate remained above 50% in 2005 (UN, 2009). Most of the countries in the region also suffer from heavy external debt burdens due to a combination of factors, including inappropriate development policies, imprudent external debt management policies, lack of perseverance in structural adjustment and economic reform, deterioration in their terms of trade, and poor governance. They have been classified as Heavily Indebted Poor Countries – HIPCs – (World Bank, 2009a).

Furthermore, the performance of agriculture in sub-Saharan Africa has been unsatisfactory, especially when contrasted with the green revolution in South Asia (World Bank, 2008). In the mid-1980s, cereal yields were comparably high. Fifteen years later in South Asia, yields had increased by more than 50% and poverty had declined by 30%. In sub-Saharan Africa, yields and poverty were unchanged. Likewise, food security remains challenging for most countries in Africa, given low agricultural growth, rapid population growth, weak foreign exchange earnings, and high transaction costs in linking domestic and international markets.

The persistence of mass poverty and hunger in this region of the world is rightly seen not only as a major ethical and political problem, but also as a serious threat to macro-economic stability and long-term development. In the wake of this threat, the international community devised the Millennium Development

Goals (MDGs), one of which is to halve extreme poverty on all its forms between 1990 and 2015. However, progress has been rather slow and even reverse. Previous estimates suggest that little progress was made in reducing extreme poverty in Sub-Saharan Africa (UN, 2008). With the recent economic downturn, major advances against extreme poverty are likely to have stalled (UN, 2009). Increases in the price of food have had a direct and adverse effect on the poor. In 2009, an estimated 55 million to 90 million more people will be living in extreme poverty than anticipated before the crisis. Likewise, the encouraging trend in the eradication of hunger since the early 1990s was reversed in 2008, largely due to higher food prices which have pushed 100 million people deeper into absolute poverty (UN, 2008). A decrease in international food prices in the second half of 2008 has failed to translate into more affordable food for most people around the world. The prevalence of hunger in developing regions is now on the rise, from 16% in 2006 to 17% in 2008. Most of this increase will occur in sub-Saharan Africa and Southern Asia, which are the poorest regions of the world.

One of the major reasons of this persistent poverty and food insecurity is the low targeting efficiency and poverty outreach of most development programs in these countries. There is a growing recognition from the development community that many existing development and safety net programs are very badly targeted (Coady and Parker, 2009). Over the past few decades, development projects failed to either reach the poor or meet their aspirations and needs in developing countries. Therefore, policy makers as well as international donors are making conscious efforts to ascertain whether the projects they fund actually reach the poor. To this end, they have begun to take concrete steps to direct their financial and technical support to those programs that have greater poverty outreach and withdraw resources from those programs that fail to reach the poor (Zeller et *al.*, 2006a). Better targeting has become an imperative for developing countries in the wake of macroeconomic and structural adjustment programs under which governments are pressured to cut back enormously on their expenditures (Chinsinga, 2005).

Moreover, the success of any development policy or project will hinge on a key factor: the extent to which they actually target and reach the poor. Excellent health or education projects make little dent in poverty alleviation if the poor fail to access them, imaginative poverty-based or income transfer policies will not have served their purpose if they are misdirected to the non-poor (Zeller et *al.*, 2006a). Ideally, targeting should help direct resources to those who need them the most, i.e. the poor. In theory, a better targeting should result in a redistribution of resources to the poor by directing resources only to them. Thus, targeting is a means of increasing program efficiency by increasing the benefit that the poor can get within a fixed budget. It allows for the most effective use of limited government and donor resources and it is likely to result in higher marginal impact given that the poor might be more efficient in using scarce resources than the less poor. Likewise, historically public spending tends to exclude the lower strata of the population. Therefore, without active efforts to target resources at the poor, even the so-called "universalist programs" will miss the poor (Grosh, 2009).

Furthermore, the literature suggests that countries with more egalitarian income distribution may perform better in terms of growth and poverty reduction than those with high income inequality (Ravallion, 1997, Thorbecke and Charumilind, 2002). Thus, better targeting may foster economic growth. Achieving the MDGs also requires targeting areas and population groups that have clearly been left behind – rural communities, the poorest households and ethnic minorities (UN, 2009).

1.2 Problem statement

By all estimates, Malawi is a very poor country with 52.4% of its population living below the poverty line and 22% living in extreme poverty (National Statistics Office – NSO – , 2005a). In other words, about 6.4 million Malawians live in poverty and as many as 2.7 million Malawians, about one in every five people, live in such dire poverty that they cannot afford to meet even their recommended daily food needs (Government of Malawi – GoM – and World Bank, 2007). The country is one of the poorest in Sub-Saharan Africa with over 80% of its workers in the primary sector, most in agriculture (Benson, 2002).

The proportion of poor people living in poverty is highest in rural areas of the southernmost (64%) and northernmost (56%) parts of the country, which are also the most densely populated rural regions, while the center is relatively less poor (47%). Urban areas have much lower percentages of people living below the poverty line (25%), and they also have the lowest share of ultra-poor (8%). Although poverty incidence rates are relatively high in most areas of the country, there is a considerable differentiation in poverty levels within districts. Nevertheless, poverty is pervasive in the country. Due to improved macroeconomic management, favorable weather conditions, and a supportive donor environment, in the last 3-4 years, the country has experienced high growth rates averaging 7.5% and the growth rate is projected at 6.9% in 2009 (World Bank, 2009c).

In the past, public services, such as agricultural extension and market infrastructure as well as resources, such as credit, fertilizer and improved seeds, etc. distributed through the existing public social safety net systems financed by international donors and the national government, were not efficiently targeted at the poor, nor to their aspirations and needs as shown by various studies (World Bank, 2006, 2007; Smith, 2001). Estimates from the IHS2 survey data of 2005 suggest that about 35% of the rural poor did not benefit from the targeted Starter Pack Initiative, also known as Targeted Input Program (TIP), whereas 62% of the rural non-poor reported benefiting from the program. Likewise, researches by Ricker-Gilbert and Jayne (2009) and Dorward et *al.* (2008) suggest that the 2006/2007 Agricultural Input Subsidy Program (AISP) has been targeted to wealthier and politically connected farmers who would otherwise have purchased the fertilizer, causing substantial displacements on the fertilizer market. Almost all social protection programs are poorly targeted in the country (GoM and World Bank, 2007).

As a result, poverty has not been reduced in the country. From 1998 to 2005, the poverty rate declined less than 2% from 54.1% to 52.4%. Moreover, extreme poverty has not substantially been reduced during the same period. However, poverty has not been static. The frequent and widespread occurrence of shocks in Malawi results in large movements into and out of poverty. Such volatility at the household level reflects the pervasive risks and shocks which affect the lives of Malawians. Recent trends in human development indicators broadly support the conclusion that there has been no or little progress in reducing poverty in the country since 1998. Furthermore, given the lack of progress during the past decade, Malawi is unlikely to achieve the target reduction in poverty and ultra-poverty by 50% between 1990 and 2015 (GoM and World Bank, 2007).

With a per capita income of US$230 (World Bank, 2008) and limited donor resources, the surplus available to redistribute is relatively small. Meanwhile, the large proportion of the population living under the poverty line means that any program large enough to have a substantial impact on the poor would be extremely costly and affordable options will only be able to reach some fairly limited portion of the population in need, and will have limited effect on household welfare (Smith, 2001). Better targeting can maximize the reduction of poverty given a limited budget for poverty alleviation and the trade-off between the number of beneficiaries covered by an intervention and the level of transfer – i.e. an opportunity cost – (Coady et *al.*, 2002). Therefore, it is important that assistance is not mistakenly given to the non-poor, who may attempt to gain access to benefits by misrepresenting their income status (Glewwe, 1992).

It has appeared that much more remains to be done or corrected to ensure that development interventions reach their intended beneficiaries in the country. A major challenge for Malawi is to develop a low cost, fairly accurate, and easy system to target the poorest (PMS, 2000). Therefore, we conduct research on the theme: *Operational Poverty Targeting by Proxy Means Tests: Models and Policy Simulations for Malawi.*

The study intends to make innovative methodological and practical contributions to the econometric estimation of poverty assessment models. Especially, we would like to establish whether indicator-based targeting offers a better prospect compared with the currently used mechanisms for targeting the poor and smallholder farmers, largely dominated by community-based targeting in Malawi. In addition to the Weighted Least Square (WLS), we employ the Weighted Logit and Weighted Quantile regressions with refined econometric methods for testing a model's robustness and out-of-sample validity. Furthermore, we estimate the cost-effectiveness and poverty impacts of targeting and assess whether using the models developed is more target- and cost-efficient than past agricultural subsidy programs, namely the Targeted Input Program (TIP) and the Agricultural Input Support Program (AISP). Hence, the development of advanced poverty models is expected to improve existing targeting methods used by the Malawian Government and donors in agricultural and rural development. Efficiently targeting the poor is likely to improve the household food security, agricultural production, and contribute to the country's overall agricultural development in the long run.

1.3 Research objectives and organization of the book

The overall objective of this research resides in developing low cost and fairly accurate models for targeting the poor and smallholder farmers and assessing the cost-effectiveness and poverty impacts of targeting in Malawi. Findings from the study should help to improve the targeting of development policies and social safety net funds towards the poor and smallholder agricultural households.

From the theoretical point of view, the research should contribute to the ongoing international research on poverty assessment and earlier works by the International Food Policy Research Institute (IFPRI), the World Bank, the Food Insecurity and Vulnerability Information and Mapping Systems (FIVIMS) of the Food and Agriculture Organization (FAO), and the project of the IRIS Center at the University of Maryland in Asia, Latin America, and Africa. Particularly, the analysis is expected to improve the above-mentioned works through the use of more refined econometric models as well as improved techniques for testing model's robustness and out-of-sample validity.

The study seeks to answer the following questions:

1. What are the best sets of indicators (models) – both in terms of accuracy and practicality – for correctly predicting whether a household is poor or not?

2. How well do the models perform out-of-sample, i.e. in an independent sample?
3. How sensitive are the models to the poverty line?
4. Is there a difference between estimation methods in terms of predictive power or targeting accuracy?
5. Is targeting by proxy means tests more target- and cost-efficient than universal interventions and community-based targeting systems?
6. What are the potential benefits and impacts of targeting by proxy means tests?

Specifically, this research seeks to achieve the following objectives:

1. identify the best sets of indicators for predicting the household poverty status;
2. perform robustness tests to assess the predictive power of the identified sets;
3. estimate the prediction intervals for the model performances;
4. evaluate the model sensitivity to different poverty lines;
5. estimate the cost-effectiveness and benefits of targeting by proxy means tests;
6. simulate the potential impacts of targeting under a proxy means test on poverty;
7. compare the model targeting efficiency to the performances of TIP and AISP programs;

This book is organized as follows. Section 1.4 reviews the literature on targeting. We address the research questions within the scope of three research articles in Chapter 2 thru Chapter 4. In the first article titled: *Operational Models for Improving the Targeting Efficiency of Development Policies: A systematic comparison of different estimation methods using out-of-sample tests* (Chapter 2), we apply two regression methods – the Weighted Least Square and Weighted Logit – along with stepwise selection of variables to develop different proxy means test models for urban and rural Malawi. Both estimation methods are compared based on their targeting performances out-of-sample and their Receiver Operating Characteristic (ROC) curves. Furthermore, the model sensitivity to the poverty line is examined and the major conclusions regarding the use of the models and its contributions to improving the targeting efficiency of Malawi's development policies are drawn.

The second paper is similar to the first one. However, in contrast to the first paper which uses continuous as well as dummy variables, the second paper titled: *Targeting the Poor and Smallholder Farmers: Empirical evidence from Malawi* (Chapter 3) uses only categorical poverty indicators and applies a stepwise logistic regression to develop simple models for identifying the poor and smallholder farmers in the country. Categorical indicators are less prone to measurement errors than continuous variables. Indicators are selected based on a set of statistical instruments, including the area under a ROC curve which is a good measure of how well an indicator predicts poverty. To facilitate the screening of beneficiaries and the models use on the field, subsequent transformations are applied after estimation and the key findings are highlighted.

The third paper which is titled: *To Target or Not To Target? The costs, benefits, and impacts of indicator-based targeting* (Chapter 4), estimates the cost-effectiveness, the benefits, and poverty impacts of targeting. It is often argued that targeting is cost-ineffective and once all targeting costs have been considered, a targeted program may not be any more cost-efficient and may not have any more effect on poverty than a universal program. We test whether this is the case for Malawi. Using a weighted Quantile regression, the paper develops proxy means test models for Malawi and assess whether targeting is more cost- and impact-effective compared with universal interventions. In addition, the potential benefits of targeting are simulated. Furthermore, we assess whether targeting by proxy indicators is more target- and cost-efficient than the 2000/2001 Targeted Input Program (TIP) and the 2006/2007 Agricultural Input Support Program (AISP), both of which were administered through community-based targeting systems and emphasize the main findings of the research.

The final chapter summarizes the main results of the study, comparing the models' performances and emphasizing their potential contributions and implications for targeting development policies in Malawi. Further research areas and the limitations of the work are also specified.

1.4 Targeting in the literature

The literature on poverty targeting is well established. By definition, targeting is the process by which benefits are channeled to the members of the high priority group that a program aims to serve (Grosh and Baker, 1995). It is a means of identifying which members of society should receive a particular benefit, such as a social transfer (Rook and Freeland, 2006). It involves two elements: first defining which categories of people should be eligible to receive benefits (i.e. setting the eligibility criteria), and second establishing mechanisms for identifying those people within the population (finding out who meets the eligibility criteria). As the main target group is the poor in this research, first we define poverty, including the profile of Malawi's poor. Then, we review the poverty targeting mechanisms often used in development practice and emphasize the use of Proxy Means Tests (PMT).

1.4.1 The concept of poverty: Theoretical considerations

1.4.1.1 Defining poverty

The concept of poverty has evolved considerably since the eighteenth century. Nonetheless, poverty is defined today as a state of long-term deprivation of well-being considered adequate for a decent life (Aho et *al.*, 2003). Poverty is also seen as a long-term phenomenon which doesn't apply to individuals in temporary need. In other words, poverty is considered as a level of consumption and expenditures by individuals in a household which has been calculated to be insufficient to meet their basic needs; the benchmark being the poverty line which is the minimum level of food and non-food consumption expenditures deemed sufficient to live a decent life. This definition of poverty is absolute and essentially monetary. It favors a certain number of basic needs (e.g. food, housing, clothing, education) that must be fulfilled before an individual can be considered non-poor.

The concept of absolute poverty is standard, but nonetheless narrow view of poverty (Benson, 2002). It defines poverty independently from individual perceptions of well-being, focuses on living standards, and relies on what decision makers judge adequate from a social point of view. Likewise, it differs from Sen's conceptualization of poverty and excludes several important components of personal and household well-being, including physical security, level of participation in networks of support and affection, access to important public social infrastructure, such as health and educational services, and whether or not one can exercise ones human rights (Benson, 2002).

According to Sen (1987), poverty is a deprivation in capabilities and functionings[1]. A functioning is an achievement (e.g. being well-nourished, educated, etc.), whereas a capability is the ability to achieve (freedom to choose, longevity, fertility, etc.). Sen (1987) emphasizes that the basic needs should be formulated in line with functionings and capabilities between which exists a simultaneous and two-way relationship. "Functionings are more related to living conditions since they are different aspects of life. Capabilities, in contrast are notions of freedom, in the positive sense: what real, but also good opportunities you have regarding the life you may lead" (Sen, 1987). Even though Sen's conceptualization of poverty has received wider attention, its empirical application is challenging. Nevertheless, some attempts have been made in the literature to incorporate Sen's views in the form of poverty indices, such as the Human Development Index (HDI) and the Human Poverty Index HPI (UNDP, 1990) which are

1 See Sen (1987) and Johannsen (2009) for further details on Sen's capability approach.

multidimensional measures of poverty and development. In sum, there is more to assessing the quality of life and the welfare of individuals than consumption and expenditures. Nonetheless, the concept of monetary poverty is widely used in economics.

Why do individuals go poor? The causes of poverty are myriad, but Aho et *al.* (2003) identify three major ones. The first refers to the unequal distribution of production factors. Countries like individuals do not have the same physical, financial, and human capital, nor do they enjoy the same access to the technological knowledge necessary for the optimal utilization of that capital. The second source of poverty stems from the choice that individuals make in allocating their time between work and leisure, spending and saving, production and consumption. According to this cause, people are responsible for their poverty because they freely choose to allocate their individual resources in certain ways and thereby assume the consequences, either positive or negative.

The third cause of poverty results from the unequal access to ways out of poverty. Therefore, improving the poor access to essential services, such as healthcare, basic education and clean water as well as access to economic opportunities, such as micro-credit and employment might help reduce poverty. Nevertheless, a country's specific context also matters in the definition of and fight against poverty.

1.4.2 Targeting the poor: Empirical methods

Targeting methods have all the same goal – to correctly identify which households or individuals should receive benefits based on predefined criteria (e.g. individuals living below the poverty line, vulnerable households, etc.) and which should not. Targeting can be based on different units, such as households or individuals. And the targeted beneficiary is not necessarily the same as the recipient (Rook and Freeland, 2006); for example a child support grant targeted at under-14s would not be given directly to the child, but to the head of the child's household.

In practice, a number of methods are used to target development interventions at the poor. The main targeting methods include means tests, proxy means tests, geographical targeting, categorical targeting, community-based targeting, and self-targeting. In the absence of targeting, program benefits are provided "universally" – In other words to everyone in the population. Table 1 gives an overview of existing targeting methods, including their advantages and weaknesses.

Table 1 is self-explanatory. A few remarks can be drawn from the Table. None of the targeting methods is perfect; all of them have advantages but also some limitations. Likewise, they are not mutually exclusive and may work better in combination if feasible. The appropriateness of targeting is determined by its costs. Divergent views on the efficacy of targeted interventions are based on differing assessments of three questions (Coady et *al.*, 2004). "Are the methods used for reaching the poor likely to achieve better targeting outcomes? Are they cost-effective? Do they raise the living standards of the poor?" Targeting is not costless. There is a whole range of costs associated with narrow targeting: administrative costs, incentive effects, private costs borne by beneficiaries, stigmatization and social discrimination, and political costs. On the other hand, universal regimes are prohibitive because of excessive leakage to the non-poor and budget constraint. Because of the special relevance of Proxy Means Tests (PMTs) for this research, we provide in the following section further details on the tests.

Table 1. Overview of poverty targeting methods

Characteristics / Targeting – methods	Definitions	Advantages	Disadvantages	Applications
Verified means tests	Aimed at the poor, based on the measurement of the beneficiary income, assets and/or nutrition status	Best way of determining eligibility, focus on the poor, reduces inclusion errors	Very costly and difficult to administer, require regular and frequent monitoring, administrative compliance results in inclusion errors, possible stigma, performance rise with country-income level, appropriate for countries with higher administrative capacity and well documented economic transactions, and programs that provide large benefits	Child support grant (South Africa), GAPVU (Mozambique)
Simple means tests	Rely on self-reported income or welfare status or qualitative assessment of a social worker with no independent verification	Simple, quick, and easy	Inaccurate, introduce perverse incentives to lie, especially when no triangulating information is collected	1980 Food Stamp Program (Jamaica)
Proxy means tests	Aimed at the poor, based more easily observable "proxy" measures of poverty (e.g. location, housing, assets) or vulnerability (e.g. household characteristics)	Focus on the poor and vulnerable, reduces inclusion and exclusion errors, can be easily replicated, fairly accurate, can guaranty horizontal equity, fairly simple training required, can be used to evaluate program outreach and impacts, system can be shared between different programs	Difficult to construct valid and accurate proxy indicators, may introduce perverse incentives to meet proxy criteria, effective verification process may be needed, may be costly and difficult to administer, especially at scale, rigid, static, possible stigma	BEAM (Zimbabwe), PAM (Zambia), INAS (Mozambique), FICHAS (Chile), PROGRESA (Mexico)
Community-based targeting	Aimed at the poor, based on community perception of poverty and vulnerability	Reflects and values local knowledge and understanding of poverty and vulnerability, simple, low administrative costs, can work in a well-defined community with good social consensus	Significant inclusion and exclusion errors, may perpetuate local patronage structures and gender bias, can be divisive, difficult to evaluate, not replicable, accuracy cannot be verified, communities often tend to modify criteria to suit their interests, diverging interests of community members, notion of community is problematic	Kalomo cash transfer (Zambia), Mchindji cash transfer (Malawi), Dowa emergency cash transfer, TIP, AISP (Malawi)

Source: Own conception and compilations from Rook and Freeland (2006), Coady et al. (2002), and Hoddinot (1999). GAPVU: Gabinete de Apoio à População Vulnerável. BEAM: Basic Education Assistance Module. PAM: Program Against Malnutrition. AISP: Agricultural Input Support Program. INAS: National Institute for Social Welfare. PROGRESA: Programa de Educacion, Salud y Alimentacion.

Table 1. Overview of poverty targeting methods (continued)

Characteristics / Targeting methods	Definitions	Advantages	Disadvantages	Applications
Categorical/ demographic targeting	Aimed at specific identifiable categories of the population associated with poverty (e.g. elders, children, female-headed households, disabled, orphans)	Easy to administer, objective/ transparent measure, high level of public support, suitable when correlation between poverty and group characteristics is strong, lower administrative costs compared with other methods	Inclusion and exclusion errors, does not necessarily target the poor and most people in need, documentation and administrative constraints may increase transaction costs for the beneficiaries	Old age pension (Lesotho), Child support grant (South Africa), Disability pension (Namibia)
Geographical targeting	Aimed at specific geographic areas with disproportionate number of poor, rarely used alone to target the poor	Easy to administer, useful as a first level targeting approach, may be more cost- efficient to concentrate resources in areas with disproportionate number of poor, can be used by all countries, useful for crisis situation and immediate needs	Inclusion and exclusion errors, can encourage migration, does not say how much resources to give to which areas, may be politically unfeasible, violate the principles of horizontal equity, leave out poor living in richer regions	Chipata cash transfer (Zambia), Social Investment Fund (Bolivia), Food subsidy (Egypt), Food-for-Education (Bangladesh)
Self-targeting[2]	Open to all, but offering benefits to which only the poor will be attracted (e.g. low wage rate), focuses on the quality of the good provided	Low administrative costs, can be linked to skill development and income generation, can generate improved infrastructure (e.g. public works), appropriate for transitory poverty, where poor and non-poor have different consumption and wage patterns	High exclusion errors, potential bias against women, those who cannot do hard physical work, can ensure good targeting but may limit the level of benefit, opportunity costs of participation, stigma, may be difficult to find a commodity that is consumed only by the poor, or not used in the livestock industry, or a wage rate that attracts only the poor, can be complex to design and administer.	MASAF public works (Malawi), Zibambele program (South Africa), EGS Maharashtra (India)
Market-delivered	Provided to all through market mechanisms (subsidies, price support)	Easy to administer	Costly and inefficient, highly regressive, excludes those who are outside the market (e.g. the poor, etc.), may distort market	Fertilizer subsidy (Malawi), price subsidies
Universal targeting	Provided unconditionally to all	Reduces costs of targeting, no exclusion errors, high level of pubic support, respects rights	High inclusion errors, too costly, cannot be sustained, especially in poor countries, low level of impacts	Basic income grant (South Africa, Namibia)

Source: Own conception plus compilations from Rook and Freeland (2006), Coady et al. (2002), and Hoddinot (1999). MASAF: Malawi Social Action Fund. EGS: Employment Guarantee Scheme.

2 Strictly speaking, all targeting methods are to some extent self-targeted because targeting always implies some actions and therefore costs for the beneficiaries in order to qualify for the program (Coady et *al.*, 2002).

1.4.3. Proxy means tests in the literature

Because of the difficulties and the costs associated with collecting and verifying detailed information on household income or consumption, especially in developing countries, governments and development institutions rely on alternative targeting methods. On such method is proxy means test.

Proxy means tests use household socioeconomic indicators to proxy its income or welfare level. As with any targeting method, the aim is to find a few indicators that are less costly to identify, but are sufficiently correlated with household income or expenditures to be used for poverty alleviation (Besley and Kanbur, 1993). These indicators are used to calculate a score that indicates how well off the household is. This score is then used to determine household eligibility to development or safety net programs (consumption and production subsidies, free food, education, health, etc.), and possibly the level of benefits. The system can also potentially be used for assessing the welfare impacts of agricultural development projects as argued by Van Bastelaer and Zeller (2006).

The first step in designing a proxy means test is to select a few variables that are well correlated with poverty and have three characteristics (Coady et *al.*, 2002): i) the variables should be few enough that it is feasible to apply the proxy means tests to a significant share of the population that may apply for the program, maybe as much as a third; ii) the variables selected must be easy to measure or observe (see for example Johannsen, 2009; Houssou et *al.*, 2007; Zeller et *al.*, 2006b; Zeller et *al.*, 2005a, b; Zeller and Alcaraz V., 2005a, b); and iii) they should be relatively difficult for the households to manipulate just to get into the program. These variables are usually available in national household surveys and Living Standard Measurement Surveys (LSMS). They often include different dimensions of poverty, such as housing, location, assets, demography, occupation, etc.

Once the variables have been chosen, statistical methods are used to associate a weight with each variable. One common approach is regression analyses, such as Ordinary Least Square (OLS), Linear Probability Model (LPM), Logit or Probit, and Quantile regressions which are used to regress household welfare measured by income or consumption on the selected variables. This procedure is often iterative in that the variables initially selected are chosen on the basis of a more comprehensive statistical analysis that evaluates their predictive power, i.e. how closely they are correlated with household welfare. Additionally, out-of-sample validations (across time and or space) are conducted when feasible, to gauge how well the system is likely to perform on the field. These tests involve the use of non-overlapping samples derived from the initial dataset or the use of datasets from different time periods to assess the predictive ability of the system (see for example Johannsen, 2009; Houssou et *al.*, 2007; Benson et *al.*, 2006; Narayam and Yoshida, 2005). Sometimes, the weights are rounded to simplify the system and facilitate calculation of scores on the field.

A key feature of proxy means test is the formulaic nature of its calculation of need. The test has the merit of making replicable judgments using consistent and visible criteria (Coady et *al.*, 2002). Proxy means tests are highly accurate and less prone to criticism of politicization or randomness. They are also less costly than verified means tests. Likewise, they are appropriate for large and long term programs, but less so for crisis situation (e.g. emergency food relief as a result of severe drought). Furthermore, the estimation methods used to develop proxy means test systems may require a high level of technological skills and may not always be well understood, especially by non-specialists. Depending on the nature of the indicators used, proxy means tests can capture only chronic or transient poverty or both.

Additional methods used to develop proxy means test models include principal component and discriminant analyses which measure relative poverty. However, a relative welfare measure only identifies the poor, but doesn't account for how much poor there are; focusing on who get program benefits, but not how much they get. Such index-based measures of poverty are useful when income or expenditures data are not available.

The efficacy of proxy means testing is demonstrated in various studies, such as Coady and Parker (2009), Johannsen (2009), Houssou et *al.* (2007), Schreiner (2006), Benson et *al.* (2006), Zeller et *al.* (2006), Narayam and Yoshida (2005), Zeller et *al.* (2005a, b), Zeller and Alcaraz V. (2005a, b), Coady et *al.* (2004), Ahmed and Bouis (2002), Baulch (2002), Braithwaite et *al.* (1999), Grosh and Baker (1995), Grosh (1994), and Glewwe and Kanaan (1989). While there is bound to be some leakage, no indicator being perfectly correlated with welfare, it is hoped that any leakage of benefits to those who are not poor is much less expensive than administering a means test or providing benefits universally to the population.

Targeting can work, but not always. In a comprehensive survey of 122 targeted antipoverty interventions, Coady et *al.* (2004) found that differences in country characteristics and implementation mechanisms are important determinants of program effectiveness than the choice of targeting method per se. For example, administrative arrangements associated with collecting and verifying information are vital to ensuring low errors of exclusion of the poor and low leakage to the non-poor. No matter how well or badly the statistical formula works, if the poor don't register for the program, it will have high exclusion errors (Coady et *al.*, 2002).

There is a long tradition of targeting by proxy means tests in Latin America. Social safety nets have long relied on proxy means tests to provide benefits to the poor (e.g. Chile's Ficha CAS, Columbia's SISBEN, and Mexico's PROGRESA). Likewise, in 2000 the U.S. Congress passed the Microenterprise for Self-Reliance and International Anti-Corruption Act which emphasized that half of all United States Agency for International Development (USAID) microenterprise funds benefit the very-poor. To meet this target, a subsequent legislation required USAID to develop and certify low cost proxy means tests tools for assessing the poverty status of microenterprise clients. Within this framework, proxy means tests are now being developed and field-tested in many developing countries.

In general, to evaluate the performances of a proxy means targeting system, a two-by-two cross-table of the actual versus predicted poverty status is used. The actual poverty status is determined by comparing the household actual expenditures to the poverty line. Households with expenditures below the poverty line are classified as poor, otherwise they are deemed non-poor. Likewise, the predicted household poverty status is determined by comparing the predictions (e.g. predicted expenditures or probability of being poor) to a benchmark (e.g. poverty line or predefined cut-off) after estimation. Table 2 illustrates the cross-classifications.

Table 2. Actual vs. predicted household poverty status

Actual poverty status	**Predicted poverty status**		
	Non-poor	**Poor**	**Total**
Non-Poor	444	104	548
Poor	105	146	251
Total	549	250	799

Source: Adapted from Zeller et al. (2006b).

Table 2 crosses the predicted versus the actual household poverty status. The results indicate that out of 548 actually non-poor households, 444 are correctly predicted as non-poor, whereas 104 are wrongly predicted as poor. Likewise, 146 of 251 truly poor households are correctly predicted as poor, whereas 105 are wrongly predicted as non-poor. Based on the above results, different performances measures are used to assess the accuracy of the system as presented in Table 3.

Table 3. Indicators of targeting performances

Accuracy ratios	Definitions
Total Accuracy	Percentage of the total sample households whose poverty status is correctly predicted by the estimation method.
Poverty Accuracy	Number of households correctly predicted as poor, expressed as a percentage of the total number of poor.
Non-Poverty Accuracy	Number of households correctly predicted as non-poor, expressed as percentage of the total number of non-poor.
Undercoverage	Number of poor households predicted as non-poor, expressed as a percentage of the total number of poor.
Leakage	Number of non-poor households predicted as poor, expressed as a percentage of the total number of poor.
Poverty Incidence Error (PIE)	Difference between predicted and actual poverty incidence, measured in percentage points.
Balanced Poverty Accuracy Criterion (BPAC)	Poverty accuracy minus the absolute difference between undercoverage and leakage, measured in percentage points.

Source: IRIS (2005).

The first three measures in Table 3 are self-explanatory. Undercoverage and leakage are exclusion and inclusion errors, respectively. They are extensively used to assess the targeting efficiency of development policies (Valdivia, 2005; Ahmed et *al.*, 2004; Weiss, 2004). In statistical terminology, undercoverage is also known as type II error or *false negative* and leakage is termed as type I error or *false positive.*

The performance measure PIE indicates the precision of a model in correctly predicting the observed poverty rate. Positive PIE values indicate an overestimation of the poverty incidence, whereas negative values show the opposite. The Balanced Poverty Acurracy Criterion (BPAC) considers three accuracy measures that are especially relevant for poverty targeting: poverty accuracy, leakage, and undercoverage. These three measures exhibit trade-offs. For example, minimizing leakage leads to higher undercoverage and lower poverty accuracy. Higher positive values for BPAC indicate higher poverty accuracy, adjusted by the absolute difference between leakage and undercoverage.

Using the results in Table 2 and the indicators in Table 3, the performances of the system can be calculated as follows:

- Total Accuracy = ((444 + 146) / 799)* 100 = 73.84%;
- Poverty Accuracy = (146 / 251)* 100 = 58.18%;
- Non-Poverty Accuracy = (444 / 548)* 100 = 81.02%;
- Undercoverage = (105 / 251)* 100 = 41.83%;
- Leakage = (104 / 251)* 100 = 41.43%;
- PIE = 31.29-31.41= -0.13 percentage points;
- BPAC = 58.18-abs(41.83-41.43) = 57.77 percentage points.

In general, actions to reduce undercoverage (e.g. raising the cut-off point) may increase the leakage rate and vice versa. Table 4 reviews the performances of selected studies (as measured by their undercoverage and leakage rates) on proxy means tests in different countries.

Table 4. Selected studies on proxy means tests

Results / Studies	Poverty rate (%)	Estimation methods	Number of indicators	Out-of-sample tests	Performances	
					Under-coverage	Leakage
Houssou et *al.* (2009)[1] Uganda	32.36	Probit	10	Yes	47.06	43.53
Iris (2008)[2] Malawi	61.4	Iterative quantile	15	Yes	16.55	17.09
Johannsen (2007) Peru	54	Weighted OLS	10	Yes	20	25.6
Schreiner (2006) India	46.37	Logit	15	No	38.5	16.1
Benson et *al.* (2006)						
Rural Malawi	54.8	OLS	17	Yes	27	34
Urban Malawi	51.6	OLS	09	Yes	18.5	25.4
Zeller et *al.* (2006b) Bangladesh	31.41	Principal component	13	No	41.83	41.43
Zeller et *al.* (2005a) Bangladesh	31.41	Iterative quantile	15	No	30.28	30.28
Zeller & Alcaraz V. (2005a) Uganda	31.4	Iterative quantile	15	No	38.04	37.65
Zeller & Alcaraz V. (2005b) Kazakstan	4.52	Iterative quantile	15	No	54.05	62.16
Zeller et *al.* (2005b) Peru	26.88	Iterative quantile	15	No	27.44	27.91

Source: Compiled from the literature. [1]*Results based on 0.5 cut-off probability.* [2]*Preliminary results.*

Table 4. Selected studies on proxy means tests (continued)

Results / Studies	Poverty rate (%)	Estimation methods	Number of indicators	Out-of-sample tests	Performances	
					Under-coverage	Leakage
Narayan &Yoshida (2005) Sri Lanka	40	OLS	34	Yes	28	31
Ahmed & Bouis (2002) Egypt	36.5	OLS	09	No	28.2	16.3
Baulch (2002)[2] Rural Vietnam	45.5	Stepwise probit	09	No	26.9	21.7
Urban Vietnam	9.2	Stepwise probit	06	No	53.3	1.9
Grosh & Baker (1995) Jamaica	30	OLS	25	No	41	34.2

Source: Compiled from the literature. [1]Preliminary results. [2] Results based on 0.5 cut-off probability.

As shown in Table 4, a number of studies have applied proxy means tests for targeting the poor in the past. Using an iterative Quantile regression with 15 indicator set in Bangladesh, Zeller et *al.* (2005a) achieve an undercoverage and leakage of about 30%. Likewise, using the OLS and a set of nine indicators for targeting food subsidies in Egypt, Ahmed and Bouis (2002) obtain an undercoverage of 28% and a leakage of 16%. However, none of the above authors validates the targeting performances out-of-sample to assess the robustness of their results; they used the same sample to fit the models and estimate the predictions.

Conversely, Narayan and Yoshida (2005) conduct out-of-sample tests based on 34 indicator set in Sri Lanka. Their results yield an undercoverage of 28% and a leakage of 31%. Similarly, Benson et *al.* (2006) achieve an undercoverage of 27% and a leakage of 34% in Rural Malawi. Differences in the number and type of variables (categorical or continuous), their practicality, the poverty rate (or poverty line applied), the estimation methods, and whether the models are validated out-of-sample or not, make difficult a systematic comparison of targeting performances across studies. Nonetheless, the general trend is that none of the studies identifies perfectly the poor. They all exhibit some targeting errors.

References

Ahmed, A. and Bouis, H. E. (2002). Weighting what's practical: *Proxy means tests for targeting food subsidies in Egypt. Food Policy*, Vol. 27, pp. 519-540.

Ahmed, A., Rashid, S., Sharma, M., and Zohir, S. (2004). Food aid distribution in Bangladesh: *Leakage and operational performance.* Discussion paper No. 173. Washington D.C.: The International Food Policy Research Institute.

Aho, G., Lariviére, S., and Martin, F. (1998). Poverty analysis manual with applications in Benin. United Nations Development Program (UNDP), Université Nationale du Bénin, Université Laval, Québec, Canada.

Baulch, B. (2002). Poverty monitoring and targeting using ROC curves: *Examples from Vietnam.* Working paper No. 161. Institute of Development Studies, University of Sussex, England.

Benson, T. Payongayong E., Ahmed A., and Sharma M. (2006). Towards operational methods in measuring absolute income poverty. Paper presented at the 26th International Association of Agricultural Economists (IAAE) Conference, Gold Coast, Australia.

Benson, T. (2002). Malawi – An atlas of social statistics. National Statistics Office and International Food Policy Research Institute, Washington D.C.

Besley, T. and Kanbur, R. (1993). The principles of targeting. *In* Including the poor, ed. M. Lipton and J. Van Der Gaag, Proceedings of a symposium organized by the World Bank and the International Food Policy Research Institute, Washington D.C.

Braithwaite, J. Grootaert, C. and Milanovic, B. (2000). Poverty and social assistance in transition countries. New York.

Chinsinga, B. (2005). The clash of voices: *Community-based targeting of safety-net interventions in Malawi. Social Policy and Administration*, Vol. 39 (3), pp. 284-301.

Coady, D. and Parker, S. (2009). Targeting performance under self-selection and administrative targeting methods. *Economic Development and Cultural Change*, Vol. 57 (3), pp. 559-587.

Coady, D., Grosh, M., and Hoddinott, J. (2004). Targeting outcomes redux. *The World Bank Research Observer*, Vol. 19, pp. 61-85.

Coady, D., Grosh, M., and Hodinott, J. (2002). The targeting of transfer in developing countries: *Review of experiences and lessons.* Washington D.C.: The World Bank.

Dorward, A., Chirwa, E., Kelly, V., Jayne, T., Slater, R., and Duncan, B. (2008). Evaluation of the 2006/07 agricultural input subsidy programme. Final report, Malawi.

Glewwe, P. (1992). Targeting assistance to the poor: *Efficient allocation of transfers when household income is not observed. Journal of Development Economics*, Vol. 38 (2), pp. 297-321.

Glewwe, P. and Kanaan, O. (1989). Targeting assistance to the poor using household survey data. Working paper No. 225. Washington D.C.: The World Bank.

Grootaert, C. and Braithwaite, J. (1998). Poverty correlates and indicator-based targeting in Eastern Europe and the Former Soviet Union. Poverty Reduction and Economic Management Network, Environmentally and Socially Sustainable Development Network. Washington D.C.: The World Bank.

Government of Malawi and World Bank (2007). Malawi poverty and vulnerability assessment report: *Investing in our future.* Synthesis report, Malawi.

Grosh, M. E. (2009). Conditional cash transfer around the world. Paper presented on April 16, 2009. Washington D.C.: The World Bank.

Grosh, M. E. (1994). Administering targeted social programs in Latin America: *From platitudes to practice.* Washington D.C.: The World Bank.

Grosh, M. E. and Baker, J. L. (1995). Proxy means tests for targeting social programs: *Simulations and speculation.* Working paper No. 118. Washington D.C.: The World Bank.

Hoddinott, J. (1999). Targeting: *Principles and practices.* Technical guide. Washington D.C.: The International Food Policy Research Institute.

Houssou, N., Zeller, M., Alcaraz V., G. Johannsen, J., and Schwarze, S. (2007). Proxy means tests for targeting the poorest households: *Applications to Uganda.* Paper presented at the 106th Seminar of the European Association of Agricultural Economists (EAAE), Montpellier, France.

IRIS. (2008). Poverty assessment tool accuracy submission. USAID/IRIS tool for Malawi, IRIS Center, University of Maryland, USA.

IRIS. (2005). Note on assessment and improvement of tool accuracy. Mimeograph, revised version from June 2, 2005. IRIS Center, University of Maryland, USA.

Johannsen, J. (2009). Operational assessment of monetary poverty by proxy means tests: *The example of Peru.* F. Heidhues, J. Braun, and M. Zeller (eds) *Development Economics and Policy 65*, Frankfurt: Peter Lang.

Narayan, A. and Yoshida, N. (2005). Proxy means tests for targeting welfare benefits in Sri Lanka. South Asia Region Working paper No. 33258. Washington D.C.: The World Bank.

National Statistics Office (2007): Malawi in figures. Annual publication of the National Statistics Office, www.nso.malawi.net (Accessed September 15, 2009).

National Statistics Office (2005a). Malawi Integrated Household Survey 2004-2005. Zomba, Malawi.
National Statistics Office (2005b). Malawi Second Integrated Household Survey (IHS2): *Basic information document.* Zomba, Malawi.
National Statistics Office (2005c). Malawi Second Integrated Household Survey: *Notes on construction of expenditure aggregate and poverty lines for IHS2.* Zomba, Malawi.
Poverty Monitoring System (2000). The state of Malawi's poor: *The incidence, depth, and severity of poverty.* Policy brief No. 2, Malawi.
Rook, J. and Freeland, N. (2006). Targeting social transfers. Regional Hunger and Vulnerability Program (WAHENGA).
Ravallion, M. (1997). Can high-inequality developing countries escape absolute poverty? *Economic Letters*, Vol. 56, pp. 51-57.
Ricker-Gilbert, J. and Jayne, T. S. (2009). Do fertilizer subsidies affect the demand for commercial fertilizer? *An example from Malawi.* Paper presented at the 27th International Association of Agricultural Economists (IAAE) Conference, Beijing, China.
Schreiner M. (2006). A simple poverty scorecard for India. Microfinance risk management, Center for social development, Washington University in Saint Louis, USA.
Sen A. K. (1987). The standard of living*: Lecture II, lives and capabilities.* Cambridge University Press, Cambridge.
Smith, J. W. (2001). Spending on safety nets for the poor: *How much, for how many? The case of Malawi.* Africa Region Working paper No. 11. Washington D.C.: The World Bank.
Thorbecke, E. and Charumilind, C. (2002). Economic growth and its socioeconomic impact. *World Development,* Vol. 30 (9), pp. 1477-1495.
United Nations (2009). Millennium Development Goals report (2009). UN, New York.
– (2008). Millennium Development Goals report (2008). UN, New York.
United Nations Development Program (1990). Human Development Report 1990: *Concept and measurement of human development.* UNDP, Rome.
Valdivia, M. (2005). Is identifying the poor the main problem in targeting nutritional program? Discussion paper No. 7. Washington D.C.: The World Bank.
van Bastelaer, T. and Zeller, M. (2006). Achieving the microcredit summit and millennium development goals of reducing extreme poverty: *What is the cutting edge on cost-effectively measuring movement across the $1/day threshold? In* Daley-Harris, Sam, and Anna Awimbo (eds). More pathways out of poverty, pp.1-31. Kumarian Press, Bloomfield, Connecticut, USA.

van de Walle, D. (1998). Targeting revisited. *The World Bank Research Observer*, Vol. 13 (2), pp. 231-248.

Weiss, J. (2004). Reaching the poor with poverty projects: *What is the evidence on social returns?* Research paper No. 61. Tokyo: The Asian Development Bank Institute.

World Bank (2009a). List of the Heavily Indebted Poor Countries. http://www.worldbank.org (Accessed September 23, 2009).

– (2009b). World Development Indicators. Washington D.C.: The World Bank.

– (2009c). Malawi – country brief. www.worldbank.org. (Accessed September 11, 2009).

– (2008). Global purchasing power parities and real expenditures 2005, International Comparison Program (ICP). Washington D.C.: The World Bank.

– (2007). Malawi social protection status report No. 40027-MW. Sustainable Development Network, Africa region. Washington D.C.: The World Bank.

– (2006). Malawi: *Public works program – conditional cash transfers as an emergency response to a national food shortage.* Washington D.C.: The World Bank.

Zeller, M., Sharma, M., Henry, C., and Lapenu, C. (2006a). An operational tool for assessing the poverty outreach performance of development policies and projects: *Results of case studies in Africa, Asia, and Latin America. World Development*, Vol. 34 (3), pp. 446-464.

Zeller, M., Houssou, N. Alcaraz V., G. Johansen, J., and Schwarze, S. (2006b). Developing poverty assessment tool based on principal component analysis: *Results from Bangladesh, Kazakhstan, Uganda, and Peru.* Paper presented at the 26th International Association of Agricultural Economists (IAAE) Conference, Gold Coast, Australia.

Zeller, M. and Alcaraz V., G. (2005a). Developing and testing poverty assessment tools: *Results from accuracy tests in Uganda.* IRIS Center, University of Maryland, College Park, USA.

Zeller, M. and Alcaraz V., G. (2005b). Developing and testing poverty assessment tools: *Results from accuracy tests in Kazakhstan.* IRIS Center, University of Maryland, College Park, USA.

Zeller, M., Alcaraz V., G., and Johannsen, J. (2005a). Developing and testing poverty assessment tools: *Results from accuracy tests in Bangladesh.* IRIS Center, University of Maryland, College Park, USA.

Zeller, M., Alcaraz V., G., and Johannsen, J. (2005b). Developing and testing poverty assessment tools: *Results from accuracy tests in Peru.* IRIS Center, University of Maryland, College Park, USA.

CHAPTER II: Targeting the poor and smallholder farmers: Empirical evidence from Malawi[3]

Abstract

The recent international financial crisis and the steady decrease in development assistance have put many poor countries under increasing pressure to target more accurately their public spending at the poor and the population in need. However, further progress is hampered by the lack of accurate and operationally reliable methods for identifying the targeted population affected by poverty. Therefore, this paper develops low cost and fairly accurate models for improving the targeting efficiency of development policies. Using household-level survey data from Malawi, this research applies various econometric methods along with out-of-sample tests to develop operational poverty targeting models for the country. Though there is a scope for further improvements, the results show that the developed models can considerably improve the poverty outreach of development policies compared with the currently used targeting mechanisms in the country. Likewise, this research can be replicated in other developing countries.

Keywords: poverty targeting, predictions, Malawi, out-of-sample tests

JEL Classification: C01, C13, I32

1. Introduction

Lately, policy makers as well as international donors have begun to take concrete steps to direct their financial and technical support to those programs that have greater poverty outreach and withdraw resources from those that fail to reach the poor. While this is definitely a step in the right direction, further progress is hampered by the lack of low cost, accurate, and operationally reliable methods for targeting the poor and assessing whether a project, policy or development institution reaches the poor and the population in need (ZELLER et al., 2006). This paper seeks to fill this knowledge gap. We develop low cost, reasonably accurate, and simple models for targeting the poor and smallholder farmers in Ma-

3 This article has been reprinted from Nazaire Houssou and Manfred Zeller (2010): Targeting the Poor and Smallholder Farmers: Empirical evidence from Malawi. *Quarterly Journal of International Agriculture (QJIA)* Volume 49 (4) pp.: 341-358, reproduced with permission from the DLG-Verlag Frankfurt/M.

lawi, one of the poorest countries in Sub-Saharan Africa with a poverty rate of 52.4% (NATIONAL STATISTICS OFFICE -NSO-, 2005a).

Deeply entrenched poverty is a major obstacle to Malawi's development and growth. The country is mostly agricultural with over 80% of its population working in the primary sector (BENSON, 2002). Though small landing holding size is not synonymous with poverty, most of Malawi's poor are smallholder farmers with 0.51 hectare of land per household. To target these poor and smallholder farmers, the Government of Malawi relies mainly on community-based targeting mechanisms in which village development committees and other community representatives identify program beneficiaries based on their assessment of the household living conditions. However, most of the country's development programs are poorly targeted at the population in need. According to the Malawi Second Integrated Household Survey (IHS2), 35% of the rural poor did not benefit from the Targeted Starter Pack (TIP)[4] of 2000/2001, while 62% of the non-poor wrongly received program benefits.

Likewise, researches by RICKER-GILBERT and JAYNE (2009) and DORWARD et al. (2008) suggest that the 2006/2007 Agricultural Input Subsidy Program (AISP) has been targeted to wealthier and politically connected farmers who would otherwise have purchased the fertilizer, causing substantial displacements in the fertilizer market. An evaluation of the AISP program indicates that 46% of the poor did not receive fertilizer vouchers, whereas 54% of the non-poor were wrongly targeted (DORWARD et al., 2008). Almost all interventions have targeting problems in the country (GOVERNMENT OF MALAWI and WORLD BANK, 2007). As a result, poverty has not been substantially reduced in the country since 1998 (NSO, 2005a). Furthermore, given the lack of progress during the past decade, Malawi is unlikely to achieve the target reduction in poverty and ultra-poverty by 50% between 1990 and 2015 (GOVERNMENT OF MALAWI and WORLD BANK, 2007).

Therefore, this research explores whether proxy means tests can improve the targeting of the poor and smallholder farmers in the country compared with the currently used methods. Proxy means tests use household socioeconomic indicators to proxy household poverty or welfare status. They have the merit of making replicable judgments using consistent and visible criteria (COADY et al., 2002) and are also simple to implement and less costly than sophisticated means tests[5]. Better targeting has become an imperative for many developing countries

4 The Targeted Starter Pack or Targeted Input Program (TIP) provided free agricultural inputs, such as fertilizers and seeds to qualified farmers.

5 Means tests directly measure household income to determine its welfare level. Due to the difficulties associated with such tests, they are largely reserved for industrialized countries. See COADY et al. (2002) and GROSH and BAKER (1995) for further details on means tests.

in the wake of structural adjustments under which Governments are under pressure to cut back enormously on public expenditures (CHINSINGA, 2005).

This paper is organized as follows. Section 2 reviews the data and methodology, whereas section 3 presents the results. Section 4 concludes the work with observations on policy implications.

2. Data and methodology

2.1 Data and theoretical framework

This research uses the Second Malawi Integrated Household Survey (IHS2) data[6]. The National Statistics Office (NSO, 2005b) of Malawi conducted the IHS2 with the assistance of the International Food Policy Research Insitute (IFPRI) and the World Bank. The survey covered 11,280 households and 51,288 individuals over an estimated population of 12,170,000 people. The sample was selected based on a two-stage stratified sampling selection which involved in the first stage the selection of the enumeration areas (EAs) based on a Probability Proportional to Size (PPS) sampling and in the second stage a random selection of 20 households per EA.

To stick with standard practice, we define poverty as a level of consumption and expenditure by individuals in a household which has been calculated to be insufficient to meet their basic needs. Furthermore, the distinction between exogenous and endogenous variables in the holistic causal chain of poverty is difficult to make in practice: feedback loops and endogeneity issues can be conceptualized virtually everywhere in this chain (GROOTAERT and BRAITHWAITE, 1998). However since the purpose of a poverty assessment is to measure poverty (i.e., to identify and use highly significant, but easily measurable correlates of poverty) and not to analyze causal relationships, it is analytically permissible to measure primary causes (lack of entitlements, rights, and endowments) together with intermediate and final outcome variables in the consumption, production, and investment spheres of individuals and their households as possible indicators of poverty (ZELLER et al., 2006). Therefore, this research does not seek to identify the determinants of poverty, but select variables that can best predict the current poverty status of a household. A causal relationship should not be inferred from the results.

---

6 We gratefully acknowledge the National Statistics Office of Malawi for providing us with the data.

2.2 Model estimation methods

2.2.1 Variable selection

Initially, about 800 variables were prepared for the estimates based on the Malawi IHS2 dataset. However, only 98 practical indicators[7] were selected for further analyses to ensure an operational use of the models. The practicality refers to two criteria: *difficulty* and *verifiability* of indicators. Initially, variables that are difficult to measure, verify (for example, subjective or monetary variables), and compute were excluded from the set of available indicators.

All of the poverty indicators used to estimate the models are categorical variables. Categorical variables are easier to measure and less susceptible to measurement error than continuous variables. Furthermore, the use of categorical variables allows simplifying the model application on the field. The list of selected variables reflects different dimensions of poverty, such as demography, housing, education, and assets. These variables are usually available in LSMS data and most national surveys in developing countries. Hence the analysis can be replicated in other countries.

2.2.2 Estimating the proxy means tests

Separate models were estimated for rural and urban areas because of substantial differences between both areas in the country. In order to perform the validation tests (confer section 2.3.2 for further details), the initial samples were first split into two sub-samples following to the ratio 67:33. The larger samples or *calibration samples* were employed to estimate the models, i.e. identify the best set of indicators and their weights, whereas the smaller samples or *validation samples* were used to test out-of-sample the predictive accuracy of the models. In the out-of-sample tests, we therefore applied the set of identified indicators and their derived weights to predict the household poverty status. We followed in the sample split a two-stage stratified sampling selection process and PPS protocol in order to mimic the initial sample selection. This design ensures that all strata are adequately represented in the calibration samples. Table 1 describes the number of indicators and the sample size by model types.

---

7 The list of indicators was reduced to 79 for the urban model; some of the variables were not relevant in urban areas.

Table 1. Sample size by model type

Sub-samples	Rural model	Urban model	Total
Total sample size	9,840	1,440	11,280
- calibration (2/3)	6,560	960	7,540
- validation (1/3)	3,280	480	3,760
Number of indicators	98	79	-

Source: Own calculations based on Malawi IHS2 data.

Except for three, all of the indicators selected are ordinal. Therefore, before estimating the models, the association of each indicator with poverty (as measured by the national poverty line) was measured by the *spearman correlation test* (SAS INSTITUTE, 2003). After performing the tests, indicators that were strongly correlated with poverty[8], including the three nominal variables were considered for further analyses. The logit regression was applied to estimate the models and identify the best set of indicators out of the preselected variables. Logit or probit regression is commonly used in the literature on poverty assessment[9]. Likewise, binary regression is the preferred choice in credit scoring (MAYS, 2004).

The models used the actual household poverty status as determined by the national poverty line of 44.29 Malawi Kwacha (MK) per day as dependent variable. This variable was coded one if the household is non-poor (i.e. expenditures above MK44.29) and zero otherwise. In other words, the logit model estimated the probability of a household being above the poverty line.

The model is specified as follows:

$$\rho_i(y_i = 1 | x_i) = \frac{1}{1 + e^{-\eta_i}} \qquad \textbf{(1)}$$

ρ_i is the probability of being non-poor, e is an exponential function, y_i is the poverty status variable, $y_i = \begin{cases} 1 \ (non\text{-}poor) \ if \ \rho_i \geq cut\text{-}off \\ 0 \ (poor), \ otherwise \end{cases}$ **(2)**

η_i is the linear predictor, $\eta_i = \beta_o + \beta_1 x_{i1} + \beta_2 x_{i2} + \ldots + \beta_k x_{ik} + \varepsilon_i$ **(3)**

8 The first fifty indicators were selected based on the absolute values of their coefficients. All of the indicators were significantly associated with poverty at 1% level of error.

9 See for example BRAITHWAITE et al. (1998); ZELLER and ALCARAZ V. (2005); ZELLER et al. (2005); SCHREINER (2006).

$x_{ik}, k = 1....K \text{ and } i = 1....n$ is the set of categorical poverty predictors, including the control variables, β_o is the intercept term, $\beta_{1k}, k = 1...K$ are the parameter estimates, ε_i is the error term.

η_i or the estimated logit is given by:

$$\ln\left(\frac{\hat{\rho}_i(y_i = 1|x_i)}{1 - \hat{\rho}_i(y_i = 1|x_i)}\right) = \hat{\beta}_o + \hat{\beta}_1 x_{i1} + \hat{\beta}_2 x_{i2} + ... + \hat{\beta}_k x_{ik} \quad \textbf{(4)}$$

A forward stepwise selection of variables was used based on the maximum "c" statistic along with judgment on potentially good poverty predictors with "c" as the area under the Receiver Operating Characteristic (ROC) curve. The higher the area of c, the higher the efficacy of the ROC to distinguish between two diagnostic situations (BAULCH, 2002). Previous applications of the "c" criterion to evaluate the accuracy of individual poverty indicators include SCHREINER (2006), BAULCH (2002), and WODON (1997) who applied the ROC curve in combination with probit or logit regression in a calibration sample only.

In addition to the "c" statistic, the criteria for the selection of indicators were based on ZELLER et al.(2006) and included practicability considerations regarding the ease and accuracy with which information on the indicators could be quickly elicited in an interview as well as considerations regarding the objectiveness and verifiability of an indicator. Likewise, variables that express similar relationships were screened to select the best. As stated by MAYS (2004), scorecard building is a combination of art and science. The policy analyst needs to exercise a good deal of judgment and common sense in evaluating the usefulness of different poverty indicators (BAULCH, 2002).

Previous researches show that in general, the higher the number of indicators, the higher the achieved accuracy[10]. Higher accuracy is often achieved at a cost of practicality and operational use. Therefore, we limited the number of regressors to the best ten set in order to balance the cost of data collection, practicality and ensure an operational use of the models[11]. Furthermore, most analysts favor the use of a maximum of ten regressors in an operational poverty targeting model. We controlled for agricultural development districts in the rural model in order to capture agro-ecological and socioeconomic differences between regions.

10 See, for example ZELLER and ALCARAZ V. (2005) and ZELLER et al. (2005).

11 The best ten simply refers to the indicator set being selected given the "c", the practicality, and the maximum number of regressors used to fit the final model. It should not be misunderstood as a value statement that implies as being best for any of the targeting ratios in Table 2.

Likewise, in the urban model we controlled for the four major cities: Mzuzu, Zomba, Lilongwe, and Blantyre.

After estimation, the model coefficients (parameter estimates) were transformed into non-negative integers in order to allow the linear predictor[12] or score to be positive and range from 0 (most likely poor) to 100 (less likely poor). Such a transformation is standard practice in credit scoring[13]. It ensures that the models developed are quick, easy, and simple to use by development practitioners, program managers, and non-specialists (see annex 3).

Having estimated a household's poverty score, the question arises as to what cut-off point to use to determine whether it is poor or not. Therefore, the score cut-off (optimal score) that maximized the BPAC (see section 2.3 for details) in the calibration sample was used to predict the household poverty status. In other words, a household is predicted as *poor* if its score is less than the optimal score cut-off and *non-poor* otherwise. This classification was crossed with the actual household poverty status. The result was then used to estimate the targeting performances of the models based on the measures described in section 2.3.

2.3 Accuracy measures and robustness tests

2.3.1. Accuracy measures

Different measures have been proposed in the literature to assess the accuracy of a poverty targeting model. This paper focuses on selected ratios which are especially relevant for poverty targeting (Table 2).

Poverty accuracy is self-explanatory. Undercoverage and leakage are extensively used to assess the targeting efficiency of development policies (VALDIVIA, 2005; AHMED et al., 2004; WEISS, 2004). Poverty Incidence Error (PIE) indicates the precision of the model in correctly predicting the poverty incidence. Ideally, the value of PIE should be zero, implying that the predicted poverty rate equals the observed rate. Positive values of PIE indicate an overestimation of the poverty incidence, whereas negative values imply the opposite. PIE is particularly useful in measuring the poverty outreach of an institution that provides microfinance or business development services.

12 The linear predictor is the log odds (equation 2). It is normally unbounded in logit models.

13 See for example SCHREINER (2006), MAYS (2004), and THOMAS et al. (2001).

Table 2. Selected accuracy ratios

Targeting ratios	Definitions
Poverty Accuracy	Total number of households correctly predicted as poor, expressed as a percentage of the total number of
Undercoverage	Error of predicting poor households as being non-poor, expressed as a percentage of the total number of
Leakage	Error of predicting non-poor households as poor, expressed as a percentage of the total number of poor
Poverty Incidence Error (PIE)	Difference between predicted and actual poverty incidence, measured in percentage points
Balanced Poverty Accuracy Criterion (BPAC)	Poverty accuracy minus the absolute difference between undercoverage and leakage, measured in percentage points

Source: Adapted from IRIS (2005).

Balanced Poverty Accuracy Criterion (BPAC) considers the poverty accuracy, undercoverage, and leakage because of their relevance for poverty targeting. These three measures exhibit trade-offs. For example, minimizing leakage leads to higher undercoverage and lower poverty accuracy. Higher positive values for BPAC indicate higher poverty accuracy, adjusted by the absolute difference between leakage and undercoverage. As mentioned earlier, the BPAC is arbitrarly used in the paper as the overall criterion to judge the model accuracy performance. In the formulation of the BPAC, it is assumed that leakage and undercoverage are equally valued. However, a policy maker may give higher or lower weight to undercoverage compared with leakage. This is possible in principle by altering the weight for leakage in the BPAC formula.

2.3.2 Assessing the predictive power of the models

Out-of-sample validation tests were performed to gauge the predictive power of the models using independent samples derived from the same population. The main purpose of the validations is to observe how well the models will likely perform when used to identify the poor on the field. Without such validations, the accuracy of the models on the field would be unknown. Therefore, the models developed were validated by applying the set of selected indicators, their weights, and the optimal score cut-offs to the validation sub-samples in order to predict the household poverty status.

Furthermore, the model robustness was assessed by estimating the prediction intervals using 1,000 bootstrapped samples. Unlike standard confidence interval estimation, bootstrap does not make any distributional assumption about the population and hence does not require the assumption of normality[14].

3. Targeting accuracy of the proxy means tests: empirical results

This section discusses the results of the estimations[15]. First, the accuracy performances of the models are presented, including the prediction intervals. Second, the ROC curves of the models are analyzed, followed by the sensitivity analyses. Finally, we explore the distribution of the model targeting errors.

3.1 Model predictive performances

Table 3 describes the model predictive performances. The poverty lines applied and the full regression results are shown in the annex. All of the coefficient estimates are highly significant. Their signs are consistent with expectations and economic theory.

Table 3 suggests that the rural model correctly identifies about 69% of the poor against 64% under the urban model. Consequently, the undercoverage is estimated at 31% for the former and 36% for the latter. These results indicate that either of the models would enable a policy maker or program manager to concentrate benefits on about 2/3 of poor households when applied in Malawi. This will maximize the effectiveness of limited resources. If, for example, the Malawian Government chooses to target all rural poor households with a cash transfer program and sets the appropriate budget, the poverty rate would be reduced by about 32% points from 47.13% to 14.84%. If it were to target only 50% of the rural poor, the poverty rate would be reduced by a sizable margin of about 16% points from 47.13% to 30.84%.

14 See HALL (1994) and EFRON (1987) for further details on bootstrapped simulation methods.

15 For brevity reasons, only out-of-sample results are presented throughout this paper.

Table 3. Model predictive performances

	Targeting ratios	Cut-off	Poverty accuracy (%)	Under coverage (%)	Leakage (%)	PIE (% points)	BPAC (% points)
Models	*Rural*	37	**68.52** (66.1; 70.6)	**31.48** (29.4 33.9)	**28.0** (25.3; 30.8)	**-1.64** (-3.5; 0.2)	**65.03** (59.7; 69.6)
	Urban	20	**63.96** (55.0; 72.3)	**36.04** (27.7; 45.0)	**36.94** (24.8; 52.0)	**0.21** (-3.5; 3.8)	**63.06** (42.9; 67.7)
Programs	*TIP*	-	**65.02**	**34.98**	**61.81**	-	-
	AISP	-	**54.00**	**46.00**	**54.00**	-	-

Source: Own results based on Malawi IHS2 data. Bootstrapped prediction intervals in brackets. PIE is defined as the Poverty Incidence Error. BPAC is defined as the Balanced Poverty Accuracy Criterion. AISP denotes Agricultural Input Subsidy Program. TIP denotes Targeted Input Program.

As concerns the inclusion error, the urban model yields a higher leakage of about 37% versus 28% under the rural model. These results indicate that a part of the benefits from e.g. a targeted transfer program would also be leaked to the non-poor as none of the models are perfect at poverty targeting. Leakage to the non-poor is not harmful per se. It may increase the politically supportable budget necessary for targeting. As stated by GELBACH AND PRITCHETT (2000), a leakier bucket may be better for redistribution to the poor whereas conversely, fine targeting can undermine political support for an antipoverty program (RAVALLION, 2007). Nevertheless, it remains to be seen whether political support for poverty reduction can be weakened in Malawi, a country where more than 50% of the population are poor.

Furthermore, both models predict the poverty rate remarkably well as their estimated PIE is very low; 0.21% and -1.64% points, respectively. The BPAC is set at 65% points under the rural model and 63% for the urban model. Compared with the rural model, the targeting performances of the urban model are low. This relatively low targeting performance may be explained by the low poverty rate in urban areas compared with rural areas: 25% versus 56%.

As concerns the bootstrapped simulations, the estimated ratios range within the prediction intervals. With respect to the rural model, the width of the prediction intervals ranges within 10% points for any given ratio at 5% level of error. This small margin suggests that the model's predictive performances are quite robust. However, the urban model displays wider prediction intervals which indicate a less robust model. This result is explained by the lower size of the sample used to validate the model[16].

More importantly, Table 3 suggests that the rural model performs better than TIP and AISP programs. For example, the model covers about 69% of the poor against 65% under TIP. Likewise, only 28% of the non-poor are wrongly targeted by the model compared with 62% for TIP.

3.2 Targeting poverty using ROC curves: examples from Malawi

As stated earlier, the cut-off that maximizes the BPAC in-sample was used to estimate the model targeting performances. Depending on administrative, budgetary, or political reasons, however a policy maker or program manager may set a different cut-off to decide on the number of poor a program or development policy should reach and ponder on the number of non-poor that would also be wrongly targeted. To demonstrate how this could be done in practice, we plot the ROC curves of the models (Figure 1).

ROC curves are powerful means for measuring the trade-offs between the coverage of the poor (poverty accuracy) and the inclusion of non-poor (inclusion error) in an operational poverty targeting model[17]. The more the ROC curve is bowed towards the upper left of the graph, the better the model predicts the actual household poverty status. To our knowledge, apart from JOHANNSEN (2009), no research has applied the ROC curve in a validation sample.

The ROC curves in Figure 1 follow the same pattern with exceptions. In general, the curves show that the higher the coverage of the poor (sensitivity), the higher the inclusion of non-poor[18]. For example, the ROC curve of the rural model indicates that covering 80% of the poor would lead to an inclusion of about 30% of the non-poor households. Extending the coverage of the poor to 90% leads to more than 40% of the non-poor being wrongly included. This pattern illustrates the challenge of targeting the poor.

---

16 Further results (not shown here) suggest that the mean and median estimates of the bootstrapped samples are very similar to the estimated targeting ratios.

17 The coverage of the poor or poverty accuracy is also known as sensitivity, whereas the inclusion of non-poor or inclusion error is also termed as 1-specificity. It is defined as the error of predicted non-poor as poor, expressed in percent of non-poor. It differs from the leakage (Table 1) which is expressed in percent of the poor.

18 The 45° line on the graph shows a ROC curve with no ranking ability. This line yields the same coverage of the poor and inclusion of non-poor at any score cut-off.

Figure 1. ROC curves of the rural model (1.) and urban model (2.)

1.

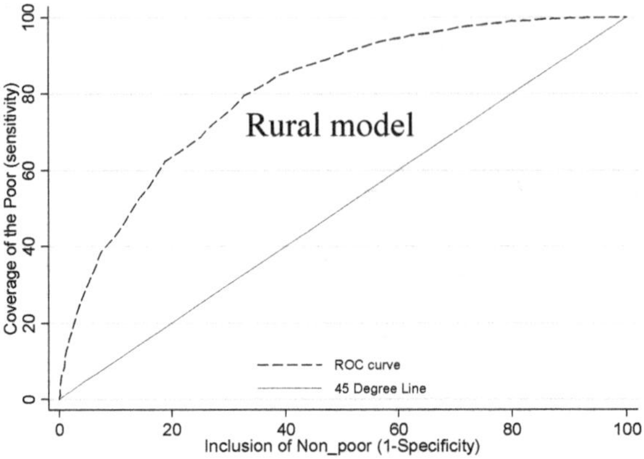

2.

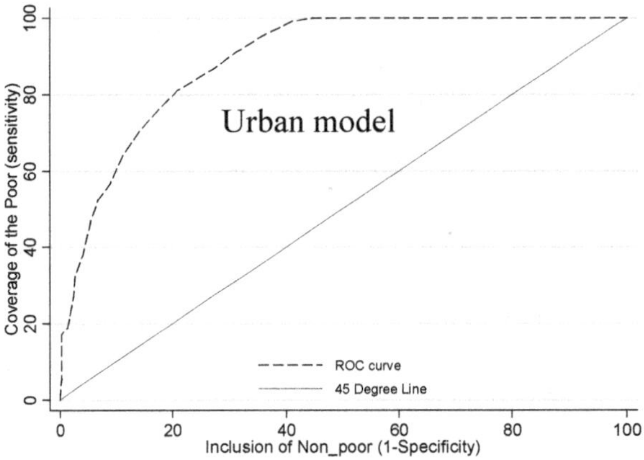

Source: Own results based on Malawi IHS2 data.

3.3 How sensitive are the models to the poverty line?

In this section, we examine the sensitivity of the models to the choice of the poverty line. These simulations involved the calibration of the models to the international and extreme poverty lines (see annex 1). Table 4 shows the results of the simulations.

Table 4. Model sensitivity to the poverty line

Targeting ratios Models	Poverty lines*	Cut-off	Poverty accuracy (%)	Under-coverage (%)	Leakage (%)	PIE (% points)	BPAC (% points)
Rural	*International*	40	**84.52** (78.8; 82.9)	**15.48** (14.0; 17.1)	**18.87** (17.0; 21.1)	**2.23** (0.6; 3.8)	**81.13** (78.9; 83.0)
	Extreme	18	**46.13** (42.3; 49.8)	**53.87** (50.2; 57.7)	**38.13** (33.3; 44.0)	**-3.54** (-5.0; -1.9)	**30.39** (21.9; 39.6)
Urban	*International*	22	**76.30** (69.9; 82.5)	**23.70** (17.5; 30.1)	**27.17** (19.2; 36.9)	**1.25** (-2.5; 5.4)	**72.83** (62.0; 77.6)
	Extreme	8	**64.71** (43.4; 80.0)	**35.29** (20.0; 52.6)	**94.12** (57.6; 152.0)	**4.17** (1.7; 7.1)	**5.88** (-52.0; 42.0)

*Source: Own results based on Malawi IHS2 data. PIE is defined as the Poverty Incidence Error. BPAC is defined as the Balanced Poverty Accuracy Criterion. Prediction intervals in brackets. *See annex 5 for description of poverty lines.*

Compared with previous results (Table 3), Table 4 shows that raising the poverty line to an international line of US$1.25 increases the coverage of the poor by about 16% points and 12% points under the rural and urban models, respectively. As a result, leakage is reduced by about 10% points for both models. The BPAC also increases by 16% points under the rural model and 19% points for the urban model. These results suggest a sizable improvement in the model targeting performances with about 85% of the poor correctly targeted in rural areas and 76% of the poor correctly identified in urban areas. Nearly, all of the poor are identified and covered in these simulations.

On the other hand, reducing the poverty line to an extreme line of MK29.31 disappointingly reduces the model targeting performances. For instance, the coverage of the rural poor is reduced by about 22% points. Likewise, leakage to the rural non-poor increases by 10% points. It seems therefore fair to conclude that the higher the poverty line, the higher the coverage of the poor (and the lower the leakage) and vice versa. The following section analyzes the model targeting performances across regions.

3.4 Spatial distribution of targeting errors

We disaggregate the model targeting errors across different regions of Malawi. Table 5 presents the distributions of these errors in rural areas.

Table 5. Spatial distribution of model targeting errors across rural Malawi

Regions **Targeting errors**	*Ka-ronga*	*Mzuzu*	*Ka-sungu*	*Salima*	*Li-longwe*	*Ma-chinga*	*Blan-tyre*	*Ngabu*
National poverty line								
Poverty rate (%)	60.00	46.56	36.00	40.12	36.72	59.84	50.16	53.33
Undercoverage (%)	26.04	35.57	31.25	20.29	35.77	52.74	11.53	14.84
Leakage (%)	11.46	28.86	35.42	46.38	42.31	6.53	34.28	40.63
International poverty line								
Poverty rate (%)	76.88	63.44	57.00	62.79	56.21	75.31	67.34	74.17
Undercoverage (%)	15.45	18.22	12.72	15.74	16.83	24.07	7.66	8.43
Leakage (%)	10.57	20.20	22.37	23.15	30.40	6.22	20.65	20.22
Extreme poverty line								
Poverty rate (%)	31.88	22.19	11.25	11.05	15.25	33.75	25.31	27.08
Undercoverage (%)	39.22	50.70	75.56	31.58	62.04	76.38	29.01	33.85
Leakage (%)	19.61	60.56	31.11	115.79	52.78	5.56	48.15	69.23

Source: Own results based on Malawi IHS2 data.

Table 5 suggests that targeting errors are not uniform across regions. Undercoverage levels are higher Mzuzu, Kasungu, Lilongwe, and Machinga, while leakage rates are higher in Ngabu, Salima, Mzuzu, Lilongwe, and Blantyre. However, error levels are lower when the model is calibrated to the international poverty line, indicating improvements in targeting performances across regions. The opposite is true with respect to the extreme poverty line. Although not reported, similar trends emerge with regard to the urban model.

4. Conclusions

This research proposes simple, low cost, and reasonably accurate models for targeting the poor and smallholder farmers using household data from Malawi. The results suggest that the developped models performs better than previous development programs targeted at the poor in the country. Likewise, findings indicate that calibrating the models to a higher poverty line improves their targeting performances, while calibrating the models to a lower line does the opposite. A key feature of the models developped is that household scores can be easily and quickly computed on the field. The best indicators selected are categorical, objective, and fairly easy to verify. However, an effective verification process (e.g. home visits, triangulation, etc.) may be needed in order to ensure a fair screening process. To reduce error levels, the models can be combined with other targeting methods. Likewise, region-specific models could also be devised for each district of the country.

The models developed can be potential policy tools for Malawi. Apart from targeting the poor and smallholder farmers, they can be used to assess household eligibility to welfare programs, measure the impacts of development policies, assess the poverty outreach of microfinance institutions, estimate the poverty rates, and monitor changes in poverty over time as the country cannot afford the costs of frequent household expenditure surveys. Though the models have proven their validity out-of-sample, there is a scope for further improvements: the observed patterns could be refined with additional validations across time as suitable data become available.

References

AHMED, A., S. RASHID, M. SHARMA and S. ZOHIR (2004): Food Aid Distribution in Bangladesh: Leakage and Operational Performance. Discussion Paper No. 173. International Food Policy Research Institute, Washington D.C.

BAULCH, B. (2002): Poverty Monitoring and Targeting using ROC Curves: Examples from Vietnam. Working Paper No. 161. Institute of Development Studies, University of Sussex, England.

BRAITHWAITE, J. C. GROOTAERT and B. MILANOVIC (2000): Poverty and Social Assistance in Transition Countries. New York.

CAMPBELL, M.K. and D. J. TORGERSON (1999): Bootstrapping: Estimating Confidence Intervals for Cost-effectiveness Ratios. In: International Journal of Medicine 92 (3):177-182.

CHEN, S. and M. RAVALLION (2008): The Developing World is Poorer than we Thought, but no less Successful in the Fight against Poverty. Policy Research Working Paper No. 4703. World Bank, Washington D.C.

CHINSINGA, B. (2005): The Clash of Voices: Community-based Targeting of Safety-net Interventions in Malawi. In: Social Policy and Administration 39 (3): 284-301.

COADY, D., M. GROSH and J. HODINOTT (2002): The Targeting of Transfer in Developing Countries: Review of Experiences and Lessons. World Bank, Washington D.C.

DORWARD, A., E. CHIRWA, V. KELLY, T. S. JAYNE, R. SLATER and B. DUNCAN (2008): Evaluation of the 2006/07 Agricultural Input Subsidy Programme. Final Report, Malawi.

EFRON, B. (1987): Better Bootstrap Confidence Intervals. In: Journal of the American Statistical Association 82 (397): 171-185.

GELBACH, J. B. and L. H. PRITCHETT (2000): Indicator Targeting in a Political Economy: Leakier can be Better. In: Journal of Economic Policy Reform 4 (2):113-145.

GOVERNMENT OF MALAWI and WORLD BANK (2007): Malawi Poverty and Vulnerability Assessment Report: Investing in our Future. Synthesis Report, Malawi.

GROOTAERT, C. and J. BRAITHWAITE (1998): Poverty Correlates and Indicator-based Targeting in Eastern Europe and the Former Soviet Union. Poverty Reduction and Economic Management Network. World Bank, Washington D.C.

GROSH, M. E. and J. L. BAKER (1995): Proxy Means Tests for Targeting Social Programs: Simulations and Speculation. Working Paper No. 118. World Bank, Washington D.C.

HALL, P. (1994): Methodology and Theory for the Bootstrap. In: http://www maths.anu.edu.au.

IRIS. (2005): Note on Assessment and Improvement of Tool Accuracy. Mimeograph, IRIS Center, University of Maryland, USA.

JOHANNSEN, J. (2009). Operational Assessment of Monetary Poverty by Proxy Means Tests: The Example of Peru. In: F. Heidhues, J. Braun, and M. Zeller (eds) Development Economics and Policy 65, Frankfurt: Peter Lang.

MAYS, E. (2004): Credit Scoring for Risk Managers: The Handbook for Lenders. South-Western Ohio, USA.

NATIONAL STATISTICS OFFICE (2005a): Malawi Integrated Household Survey 2004-2005. Zomba, Malawi.

NATIONAL STATISTICS OFFICE (2005b): Malawi Second Integrated Household Survey (IHS2): Basic Information Document. Zomba, Malawi.

SAS INSTITUTE (2003): The Logistic Procedure: Effect Selection Methods. Cary, N.C., USA.

SCHREINER, M. (2006): A Simple Poverty Scorecard for India. Microfinance Risk Management, Center for Social Development, Washington University in Saint Louis, USA.

RAVALLION, M. (2007): How Relevant is Targeting to the Success of an Anti-poverty Program? Policy Research Working Paper No. 4385. World Bank, Washington D.C.

RICKER-GILBERT, J. and T. S. JAYNE (2009): Do Fertilizer Subsidies Affect the Demand for Commercial Fertilizer? An Example from Malawi. Paper Presented at the 27th International Association of Agricultural Economists (IAAE) Conference, Beijing, China.

THOMAS, LC. J. BANASIK and JN. CROOK (2001): Recalibrating Scorecards. In: Journal of Operational Research Society 52 (09): 981-988.

VALDIVIA, M. (2005): Is Identifying the Poor the Main Problem in Targeting Nutritional Program? Discussion Paper No. 7. World Bank, Washington D.C.

WEISS, J. (2004): Reaching the Poor with Poverty Projects: What is the Evidence on Social Returns? Research Paper No. 61. Asian Development Bank Institute, Tokyo.

WODON, Q. (1997): Targeting the Poor using ROC Curves. In: World Development 25 (12): 2083-2092.

WORLD BANK (2008): Global Purchasing Power Parities and Real Expenditures 2005, International Comparison Program (ICP). World Bank, Washington D.C.

ZELLER, M., M. SHARMA, C. HENRY and C. LAPENU (2006): An Operational Tool for Assessing the Poverty Outreach Performance of Development Policies and Projects: Results of Case Studies in Africa, Asia, and Latin America. In: World Development 34 (3): 446-464.

ZELLER, M. and V. G. ALCARAZ (2005): Developing and Testing Poverty Assessment Tools: Results from Accuracy Tests in Uganda. IRIS Center, University of Maryland, USA.

ZELLER, M., V. G. ALCARAZ and J. JOHANNSEN (2005): Developing and Testing Poverty Assessment Tools: Results from Accuracy Tests in Bangladesh. IRIS Center, University of Maryland, USA.

Annexes

Annex 1. Malawi's poverty rates by region and poverty line

Types of poverty lines	Poverty lines (MK*)	Poverty rate (in percent of people)			Poverty rate (in percent of households)		
		national	rural	urban	national	rural	urban
Extreme	29.81	26.21	28.66	8.72	19.94	22.08	5.95
National	44.29	52.40	56.19	25.23	43.58	47.13	19.67
International	59.18 (US $1.25 PPP)	69.52	73.59	40.26	61.04	65.20	33.08

Source: Own results based on Malawi IHS2 data, Chen and Ravallion (2008), and World Bank (2008). MK denotes Malawi Kwacha or national currency. PPP stands for Purchasing Power Parity.

Annex 2. Results of the maximum likelihood estimates (rural model)[19]

Likelihood ratio: 950419.735***	Wald Chi-square: 554730.601***
Score: 781671.495*** c-statistic = 0.837	Number of observations = 6560

Parameters	Estimates	Standard Error	Wald Chi-Square	Pr > ChiSq	Exp(Est)
Intercept	1.5498	0.0212	5340.5537	<.0001	4.710
Agricultural development district is Karonga	-0.1775	0.00817	472.2879	<.0001	0.837
Agricultural development district is Mzuzu	0.0643	0.00568	128.4419	<.0001	1.066
Agricultural development district is Kasungu	1.0299	0.00521	39023.5476	<.0001	2.801
Agricultural development district is Salima	0.0552	0.00592	87.0985	<.0001	1.057
Agricultural development district is Lilongwe	0.6642	0.00365	33125.4007	<.0001	1.943
Agricultural development district is Machinga	-0.7539	0.00381	39207.3345	<.0001	0.471
Agricultural development district is Blantyre	-0.4910	0.00385	16292.7820	<.0001	0.612
Agricultural development district is Ngabu (reference)					
Household size is two or less	2.7505	0.00473	337670.576	<.0001	15.651
Household size is three	0.8489	0.00355	57039.3650	<.0001	2.337
Household size is four	0.1165	0.00338	1186.4186	<.0001	1.124
Household size is five	-0.6271	0.00357	30914.1938	<.0001	0.534
Household size is six or seven	-1.1727	0.00345	115519.285	<.0001	0.310
Household size is eight or more (reference)					
Household head sleeps on bed and mattress	0.5739	0.00543	11175.4626	<.0001	1.775
Household head sleeps on bed and mat/bed alone	0.2921	0.00503	3372.9606	<.0001	1.339
Household head sleeps on mattress on the floor	0.0541	0.00749	52.2385	<.0001	1.056
Household head sleeps on mat (grass on the floor)	-0.2226	0.00379	3457.2988	<.0001	0.800
Household head sleeps on cloth/sack/floor (reference)					
Maximum class level ever attended by members is primary/nursery	-0.8112	0.0186	1901.2740	<.0001	0.444
Maximum class level ever attended by members is secondary	-0.2251	0.0186	146.6400	<.0001	0.798
Maximum class level ever attended by members is training/college	0.6733	0.0273	607.8646	<.0001	1.961
Maximum class level ever attended by members is university (reference)					
Household head owns no bicycle	-0.2754	0.00185	22265.7807	<.0001	0.759
Household head owns a bicycle (reference)					
House lighting fuel is collected firewood/grass	-0.9111	0.0114	6415.8002	<.0001	0.402
House lighting fuel is purchased firewood	-0.9687	0.0277	1224.5835	<.0001	0.380
House lighting fuel is candle	0.6149	0.0268	527.8702	<.0001	1.849
House lighting fuel is paraffin/diesel	-0.2468	0.0105	550.5214	<.0001	0.781
House lighting fuel is battery/dry cell/electricity (reference)					
House flooring material is sand	-0.6056	0.00626	9357.2213	<.0001	0.546
House flooring material is smooth mud/wood	-0.0747	0.00364	420.6285	<.0001	0.928
House flooring material is tile or cement (reference)					
Household owns no tape/cd player/HiFi	-0.2987	0.00274	11882.2099	<.0001	0.742
Household owns a tape/cd player/HiFi (reference)					
No household member sleeps under a bed net	-0.2096	0.00188	12378.3402	<.0001	0.811
A household member sleeps under a bed net (reference)					
Household grew no tobacco in the past five years	-0.2158	0.00221	9503.7619	<.0001	0.806
Household grew tobacco in the past five years (reference)					
Household head cannot read in Chichewa language	-0.1562	0.00178	7673.3451	<.0001	0.855
Household head can read in Chichewa language (reference)					

*Source: Own results based on Malawi IHS2 data. *** denotes significant at the 99% level. ** denotes significant at the 95% level.*

19 The results of the urban model are available upon request.

Annex 3. Malawi's rural poverty model calibrated to the national poverty line[20]

Indicators	Values	Weight	Score
1. Where does the household live (agricultural development district)?	Blantyre	0	
	Ngabu	1	
	Karonga	2	
	Salima, Mzuzu	4	
	Linlongwe, Machinga	8	
	Kasungu	10	
2. How many people live in the household?	Eight or more	0	
	Six or seven	5	
	Five	9	
	Four	14	
	Three	18	
	Two or less	31	
3. What does the household head sleep on?	Floor/clock or sack on the floor	0	
	Mat (grass) on the floor	3	
	Mattress on floor	5	
	Bed alone/Bed & Mat (grass)	7	
	Bed & Mattress	8	
4. Does the household own a bicycle?	No	0	
	Yes	4	
5. What is the maximum class level attended by household members?	Nursery/Primary	0	
	Secondary	4	
	University	8	
	Training/College	10	
6. What is the household source of lighting fuel?	Collected/purchased firewood or grass	0	
	Paraffin/diesel	5	
	Candle	11	
	Electricity, gas or battery/dry cell	17	
7. What is the house flooring material made of?	Sand	0	
	Smooth mud/wood	4	
	Smooth cement/tile	9	
8. Does any household member sleep under a bed net?	No	0	
	Yes	3	
9. Did the household grow tobacco in the past five cropping seasons?	No	0	
	Yes	3	
10. Does the household own a tape/cd player, or HiFi?	No	0	
	Yes	4	
11. Can the household head read in Chichewa language?	No	0	
	Yes	2	
Household is deemed poor if its total score is less than 37		Total score	
Household poverty status: Poor ☐ Non-poor ☐			

Source: Own results based on Malawi IHS2 data.

20 The results of the urban model are available upon request.

CHAPTER III: Operational Models for Improving the Targeting Efficiency of Development Policies: A systematic comparison of different estimation methods using out-of-sample tests[21]

Abstract

There is a long standing belief that accurate targeting of the poor can improve the effectiveness of development policy. While a number of factors, such as governance failure, inadequate targeting methods, political interference, or lack of political will, might explain low targeting efficiency, this paper focuses on improving indicator-based models that identify poor households more accurately.
Using stepwise regressions along with out-of-sample validation tests, this paper develops proxy means test models for rural and urban Malawi. The models developed have proved their validity and can therefore be used to target a wide range of development policies in the country. Likewise, the research here can be extended to other developing countries.

1. Introduction

There is a long standing belief that development policy can be more effective with improvements to the mechanisms that target the poor. Many pro-poor programs fail to target accurately, resulting in a large proportion of program benefits leaking to higher-income groups, whereas a substantial proportion of the poor are excluded (Coady and Parker, 2009). Low targeting efficiency can impede the efforts to reduce food insecurity and poverty in many developing countries. Achieving the Millennium Development Goals (MDGs) also requires effective targeting of population groups that have clearly been left behind: rural communities, the poorest households and ethnic minorities (United Nations – UN, 2009).

Malawi is one of the poorest countries in Sub-Saharan Africa with a poverty rate of 52.4% (National Statistics Office, 2005). In response to widespread poverty and endemic food insecurity, the country's policymakers enacted various development and safety net programs, such as free or subsidized food, education,

21 This article has been reprinted from Nazaire Houssou and Manfred Zeller (2012): Operational Models for Improving the Targeting Efficiency of Development Policies A systematic comparison of different estimation methods using out-of-sample tests. *European Journal of Development Research (EJDR)* Volume 24 (3) pp.: 465-490, reproduced with permission from Palgrave Macmillan.

health, cash-for-work, input subsidies, and input-for-work (see, for example, World Bank, 2007) which targeted the poor. Most of these previous programs relied mainly on community-based targeting systems in which local authorities, village development committees, and other community representatives identified program beneficiaries in the population[22]. This process is characterized by poor targeting due to a number of factors, including various local perceptions, favoritism, a lack of understanding of targeting criteria, political interests, poor implementation, etc. A survey of previous targeted programs, including free food, input-for-work, targeted input and food/cash-for-work based on the Malawi Second Integrated Household Survey (IHS2) data of 2005, suggests that on average 73% of the poor did not receive targeted benefits, whereas 27% of the non-poor were wrongly targeted. These results are also consistent with the Government of Malawi (GoM) and World Bank (2007) who report that most of Malawi's social protection programs are poorly targeted.

In the last 3-4 years, Malawi has experienced high economic growth rates averaging 7.5% per year through improved macroeconomic management, favorable weather conditions, and a supportive donor environment (World Bank, 2009b); however, between 1998 and 2005, the country's poverty rate dropped less than 2 percentage points – from 54.1% to 52.4% (GoM and World Bank, 2007). While the level of funding for different programs is not necessarily inadequate (World Bank, 2007), existing statistics indicate that food insecurity remains rampant (Chinsinga, 2005). Observers, such as the World Bank (2007) and the Poverty Monitoring System (2000), acknowledge that more needs to be done to ensure that targeted programs effectively reach the poor.

Therefore, we seek to determine whether proxy means tests can more effectively identify and target the poor in Malawi. Instead of asking about incomes directly, proxy means tests use household socioeconomic indicators to measure the poverty or welfare level of a household. The tests are a simplification of the relationships often seen between household characteristics and its welfare level (Benson *et al.*, 2006). In general, proxy means tests use a few indicators that can be easily verified and sufficiently correlate with income to be useful for targeting the poor (Besley and Kanbur, 1993). They have the merit of making replicable judgments using consistent and visible criteria (Coady *et al.*, 2002). They are also simple to implement and less costly than verified means tests which rely on direct measurements of income to estimate a household's means of living or welfare level. Verified means tests are appropriate for developed countries where in-

22 See Chinsinga (2005) and Levy and Barahona (2002) for further details on community-based targeting.

come records are well documented[23]. Proxy means tests can address the difficulty associated with collecting and verifying income in developing countries by using objective and easily verifiable indicators that correlate with income or expenditures in nationally representative survey data.

To identify the best set of indicators for correctly predicting a household's poverty status, we apply the Weighted Least Square (WLS) and the Weighted Logit (WL) estimation methods using stepwise selection routines to select the indicators. The predictive power and robustness of the estimation methods are compared using out-of-sample tests and Receiver Operating Characteristic (ROC) curves. The prediction intervals of the estimation methods' performances are estimated using the bootstrap algorithm. The sets of variables used in the models are objective and fairly easy to verify. Moreover, they are usually available in Living Standard Measurement Survey (LSMS) and national survey data in developing countries. Hence, this research can be extended to other countries. This paper is organized as follows: Section 2 provides the methodology, Section 3 presents the results with applications to household data from Malawi, and Section 4 offers our concluding remarks.

2. Data and estimation methods

2.1 Data

We use the data gathered from the Second Malawi Integrated Household Survey (IHS2) which was conducted by the Malawi NSO (National Statistics Office, 2005) with assistance from the International Food Policy Research Institute (IFPRI) and the World Bank[24]. The IHS2 was carried out from March, 2004 to March, 2005 and covered a nationally representative sample of 11,280 households selected by a two-stage stratified sampling design. The first stage of the design selected 564 Primary Sampling Units (PSU) based on Probability Proportional to Size (PPS) sampling while the second stage was a random selection of 20 households per PSU.

The IHS2 is particularly appropriate for our research for three reasons. First, it used an improved methodology (e.g., United Nations Classification of Individual Consumption According to Purpose – COICOP) to collect and compute household consumption expenditures. Second, the survey covered a wide range of

23 See Coady *et al.* (2002) and Grosh and Baker (1995) for further details on means tests.

24 We gratefully acknowledge the National Statistics Office of Malawi (NSO) for providing us with the data.

poverty indicators that are potentially suitable for developing proxy means test models. Third, the sample is representative at national as well as district levels.

In this research, we define poverty as a level of consumption and expenditures insufficient to meet individual basic needs in a household. It is generally agreed among analysts that expenditures (as an income proxy) are a more robust measure of poverty than income itself (Deaton, 1997). This is a standard, but nonetheless narrow definition of poverty (Benson, 2002). In view of the widespread use of monetary poverty lines with expenditure-based measures of poverty, however, this research pursues a policy-relevant objective by identifying indicator-based tools that can simplify the identification of the poor and measure welfare changes over time in poor populations.

2.2 Model estimation methods

2.2.1 Poverty predictors and sample selections

The set of poverty predictors used in the rural model includes 148 indicators[25] that were selected based on their practicality, a prerequisite for the operational use of the models. Practicality refers to two criteria: *difficulty and verifiability of indicators.* Difficulty can be expressed in terms of time, money, and social costs expended for obtaining information. For example, the value of total assets is very difficult and tedious to obtain, and therefore is not really suitable for an operational poverty assessment model. With regard to the verifiability criterion, the indicators selected must be objective – i.e., characterized by measurement scales that can be, at least in principle, verified by consistent standards of measurement metrics. In keeping with the practicality criteria, variables that do not meet these requirements were excluded from the set of available indicators.

Before estimating the regressions, the initial list of variables was screened for multicollinearity within dimensions based on Variance Inflation Factors (VIF) and correlation analyses. First, bivariate correlation analyses of ratio-scale variables were run within variable dimensions (e.g., education, demography, housing, assets, etc.). To stick with standard practice, variables deemed less practical were dropped between pairs of variables with estimated correlation coefficients above 0.8. Furthermore, the reduced variable list was submitted to separate regressions within dimension with per-capita daily expenditures as the dependent variable. Following Gujarati (2003), variables with a VIF above 10 were re-

25 The list of indicators was reduced to 112 for the urban model as some of the variables were not relevant in urban areas.

moved from the set. The final variable list includes 134 indicators in the rural model. The screening of poverty indicators based on VIF and correlation analyses is the first step toward the selection of indicators significantly associated with poverty.

Separate models were estimated for rural and urban households for two main reasons. First, Malawi's poverty report revealed different profiles for urban and rural households (see, for example, the National Statistics Office, 2005). Second, interactions between the regions and other variables were found to be statistically significant in a national-level model.

To perform the validation tests, each sample was first split into two subsamples following the ratio 67:33, or 2/3 – 1/3. The larger sample or *calibration sample* was used to estimate the models, whereas the smaller sample or *validation sample* was employed to test the predictive accuracy of the models out-of-sample. In other words, after estimating the model, the set of identified indicators and their derived weights were applied to the validation sample to predict the household poverty status. To mimic the initial sample selection, we used a two-stage stratified sampling and PPS protocol in the sample split. In other words, we first selected the PSUs from each stratum (district) based on PPS with a rate of 82% (i.e., the square root of 2/3). Second, we selected the households from each PSU independently based a simple random sampling with a rate of 82%. The square of the rate amounts to 2/3 of observations in the initial sample. The remaining observations (1/3) were used as the validation sample. This design ensures that all strata are adequately represented in the calibration samples. A simple random sampling split would not guarantee such representativity.

The 67:33 split put more emphasis on model calibration than validation. Furthermore, the continued representativity of the calibration samples was assessed by testing the differences in estimates between the samples and the full datasets. Test results indicate no statistically significant difference between both sets. Therefore, the calibration samples enjoy the same representativity as the full datasets. After performing the sample splits, household weights were readjusted to reflect the true inflation rates in the calibration samples. Following the National Statistics Office (2005), the new weights were calculated by dividing the total household population in each stratum by the number of selected households in the stratum. Since the weights are not necessary to assess the out-of-sample accuracy of the models, we did not apply any weights to the validation samples. Annex 1 describes the sample sizes and the number of indicators by model type.

2.2.2 Estimation methods

Two methods were applied to estimate the models: the Weighted Least Square (WLS) and the Weighted Logit (WL) regressions. Both regressions were scaled according to the household weight, which determines how much each observation in the dataset influences the final parameter estimates of the population. Weighted regressions are appropriate in the presence of non-self-weighted random samples[26].

WLS and WL regressions are widely used in the literature; however, there is a debate on the merits of welfare regressions versus binary poverty models (Braithwaite *et al.*, 2000). WLS uses the full information available by estimating the model over the entire welfare spectrum, whereas WL collapses the entire expenditure distribution into two categories[27]. There is also a Maximum Likelihood underpinning the WLS based on the errors following a normal distribution. Combined with the use of a poverty line to identify the poor (see Section 2.2.3) in the WLS case, the differences between the two regression methods appear smaller. Likewise, the WLS and WL models are restrictive because both models assume a linear welfare model and a specific distribution of errors in that model (see, for example, Ravallion, 1996).

In addition to estimating a welfare model, Braithwaite *et al.* (2000) use a binary poverty model in their regressions after suspecting the possibility of systematic measurement errors in their data. These authors also add that it is a judgment call whether the loss of information embodied in the binary regression outweighs the risk of bias due to measurement errors. Here, we would like to emphasize that the main issue is not the measurement errors in the dependent variable per se, but the correlation between these errors and the explanatory variables as some of these variables are correlated with wealth or the type of income-generating activity. This correlation would plausibly link the explanatory variables to the size of the error in measuring welfare. In this paper, we systematically compare the targeting performances of WLS and WL methods to derive the best method for targeting the poor and improving the efficiency of development policies.

---

26 Indeed, the initial sample is self-weighted; however, household replacements for various operational reasons during the survey period resulted in a non-self-weighted random sample which justifies the use of weighted regressions.

27 For example Grosh and Baker (1995) argue that strictly speaking, ordinary least square is not appropriate for predicting poverty. Glewwe (1992) and Ravallion and Chao (1989) try to solve the problem of targeting using more complex poverty minimization algorithms. These methods are, however, difficult to implement and have limited applications compared with the methods used in this paper.

The WLS regression used the continuous dependent variable logarithm of per-capita daily expenditures[28], whereas the dependent variable in the WL regression was the actual household poverty status as a dummy variable, coded one if the household is poor (i.e., expenditures were below the national poverty line) and zero if otherwise. In other words, the WL method estimates the probability of a household being below the poverty line. Both methods sought to identify the best set of ten indicators for predicting household poverty status. Previous research shows that including more than ten regressors only generates marginal gains in accuracy, while increasing the number of indicators and thereby the complexity of the model (see, for example, Johannsen, 2009; Zeller and Alcaraz V., 2005; and Zeller *et al.*, 2005). Although not reported in this paper, our own results seem to concur as they show that increasing the number of regressors beyond ten yields only marginal gains in accuracy. Therefore, we limited the number of indicators to the best ten in order to balance the model's accuracy with its practicality/costs of implementation.

A model with a high explanatory power is a prerequisite for good predictions of the dependent variable, per-capita daily expenditures, and thereby poverty status. Therefore, the best ten regressors used for estimating the WLS regression were selected based on the stepwise MAXR (Maximum R-square) routine of SAS (SAS Institute, 2003) that seeks to maximize the method explained variance (i.e., R^2). The MAXR routine considers all combinations among pairs of regressors to move from one step to the next. In the first step, the MAXR method begins by finding the one-variable model producing the highest R^2. In the second step, another variable, the one which yields the greatest increase in R^2, is added. Once the two-variable model is obtained, each of the variables in the model is compared with each of the variables not in the model. For each comparison of single pairs of variables, the MAXR method demonstrates whether removing one variable and replacing it with the other variable increases R^2. After comparing all possible switches, the MAXR routine makes the switch that produces the largest increase in R^2. Comparisons then begin again in the third step and the process continues until the MAXR routine finds that no switch can increase R^2. The final number of variables selected, N, is determined by the MAXR routine itself; however, we set N at ten variables as stated earlier.

With regard to the WL regression, the best ten regressors were selected using the Stepwise Score routine of SAS which is similar to the MAXR routine, offering a method for best subset selection of variables with logistic regressions. The

---

27 The logarithm of expenditures was used instead of simple expenditures because the log function better approximates a normal distribution.

stepwise score routine seeks the best set of variables that maximizes the likelihood score (chi-square) statistic[29].

To capture agro-ecological and socioeconomic differences between regions, we controlled for agricultural development districts in the rural model. This also captures the effects of omitted variables as well as the effects of other unobservable factors in the model. Likewise, in the urban model we controlled for the four major cities: Mzuzu, Zomba, Lilongwe, and Blantyre. Although the inclusion of geographical dummy variables improves the model fit, it implies that two households with identical scores in all the other variables may be discriminated against solely on the basis of their place of residence. This is a politically sensitive issue which also raises ethical concerns. Therefore, the application of the method to any targeted intervention requires some flexibility in the selection process.

Using the calibration samples, we estimated both models following Greene (2003) and Wooldridge (2006):

- *Weighted Least Square*

$$y_i = \beta_o + \beta_1 x_{i1} + \beta_2 x_{i2} + \ldots + \beta_k x_{ik} + \varepsilon_i \qquad \textbf{(1)}$$

where y_i is the logarithm of daily per-capita expendit $x_{ik}, k = 1....K \ and\ i = 1....n$ ures, are the set of poverty predictors, including the control variables, β_o is the intercept term, $\beta_k, k = 1...K$ are the parameter estimates, ε_i is the random disturbance, and n is the total number of observations in the sample. The predicted value of y_i, $\hat{y}_i$, is estimated by:

$$\hat{y}_i = \hat{\beta}_o + \hat{\beta}_1 x_{i1} + \hat{\beta}_2 x_{i2} + \ldots + \hat{\beta}_k x_{ik} \qquad \textbf{(2)}$$

A weighted sum of residual squares is minimized to obtain the parameters as follows: $\min \sum_{i=1}^{n} \omega_i (y_i - \hat{y}_i)^2$ **(3)**

where $\omega_i, \imath = 1...n$ is the weight of observation i in the population.

- *Weighted Logit*

$$\rho_i(z_i = 1 | x_i) = \frac{1}{1 + e^{-\eta_i}} \qquad \textbf{(4)}$$

---

27 See SAS Institute (2003) for further details on the score procedure.

where ρ_i is the probability of being poor, e is an exponential function, and z_i is the poverty status variable:

$$z_i = \begin{cases} 1\ (poor)\ if\ \rho_i \geq cut-off \\ 0\ (non-poor),\ otherwise \end{cases} \quad \textbf{(5)}$$

η_i is the linear predictor:

$$\eta_i = \alpha_o + \alpha_1 x_{i1} + \alpha_2 x_{i2} + \ldots + \alpha_k x_{ik} + \varepsilon_i \quad \textbf{(6)}$$

where $x_{ik}, k = 1 \ldots . K\ and\ i = 1 \ldots . n$ are the set of poverty predictors, including the control variables, α_o is the intercept term, $\alpha_{1k}, k = 1 \ldots K$ are the parameter estimates, and ε_i is the random disturbance. The estimated logit or natural log ($\ln$) of the odds is given by:

$$\ln\left(\frac{\hat{\rho}_i(z_i = 1|x_i)}{1-\hat{\rho}_i(z_i = 1|x_i)}\right) = \hat{\alpha}_o + \hat{\alpha}_1 x_{i1} + \hat{\alpha}_2 x_{i2} + \ldots + \hat{\alpha}_k x_{ik} \quad \textbf{(7)}$$

A weighted Maximum Likelihood Estimator (MLE) is maximized to obtain the parameters as follows:

$$MLE = \max \sum_{i=1}^{n} \omega_i \left[\left\{ z_i \ln\left(\frac{1}{1+e^{-\hat{\eta}_i}}\right) \right\} + \left\{ (1-z_i) \ln\left(1 - \frac{1}{1+e^{-\hat{\eta}_i}}\right) \right\} \right] \quad \textbf{(8)}$$

where $\omega_i, i = 1 \ldots n$ is the weight of observation i in the population.

As stated hitherto, the estimated models are simplifications of reality as they do not encompass the myriad of essentially random aspects of economic life (Greene, 2003). Likewise, a distinction between exogenous and endogenous variables in the holistic causal chain of poverty is difficult to establish in practice: feedback loops and endogeneity issues can be conceptualized virtually everywhere along the chain (Grootaert and Braithwaite, 1998). However, the purpose of a poverty assessment tool is to predict poverty (i.e., to identify and use highly significant but easily measurable correlates of poverty) – not to analyze causal relationships. Therefore, it is analytically permissible to measure primary causes (lack of entitlements, rights, and endowments) together with intermediate and final outcome variables in the consumption, production, and investment spheres of individuals and their households as possible indicators of poverty

(Zeller *et al.*, 2006). The estimated models do not seek to identify the determinants of poverty, but rather are intended to select variables that can best predict the current poverty status of a household. A causal relationship should not be inferred from the results.

Nonetheless, possible endogeneity may limit the usefulness of the model across samples. If some of the explanatory variables are indeed endogenous, then the resulting coefficients will be biased because of the correlation of those variables with the errors. This may not significantly alter the predictive power of the calibrated model as long as the correlation pattern is maintained, however, changes in the correlation (due to different sampling procedures, differences in measurement or the application of the explanatory variables to areas where the endogenous channel is more or less strong) will mean that the estimated coefficients are not only biased with respect to the true causal model, but are also biased with respect to partial correlations.

2.2.3 Predicting the household poverty status

Having estimated the models, the question arises as to what cut-off to use for classifying the household as poor and non-poor. We explored three classifications using different cut-offs: national, percentile-corrected, and maximum-BPAC cut-offs. The first and most obvious classification compared the predicted expenditures to the national poverty line of 2005 (IHS2, 2005). Households with predicted expenditures less than MK44.29 were classified as poor, otherwise they were deemed non-poor. This poverty line determines the actual poverty rate in the population. Similarly, the probability of being poor was compared with the cut-off point (predicted probability) that determined the actual poverty rate in the population. Households whose predicted probability was higher than this cut-off point were classified as poor, otherwise they were deemed non-poor.

However, the above classification ignores random disturbance in the estimation of both regressions which may result in biased estimates of poverty rates (Hentschel *et al.*, 2000) and thereby targeting performances. Therefore, a second classification based on the percentile-corrected poverty line (PC) was used[30]. Figure 1 illustrates the national and percentile-corrected poverty lines.

30 See Johannsen (2009) for further details on the percentile-corrected approach.

Figure 1: Cumulative distribution of poverty rate (rural model).

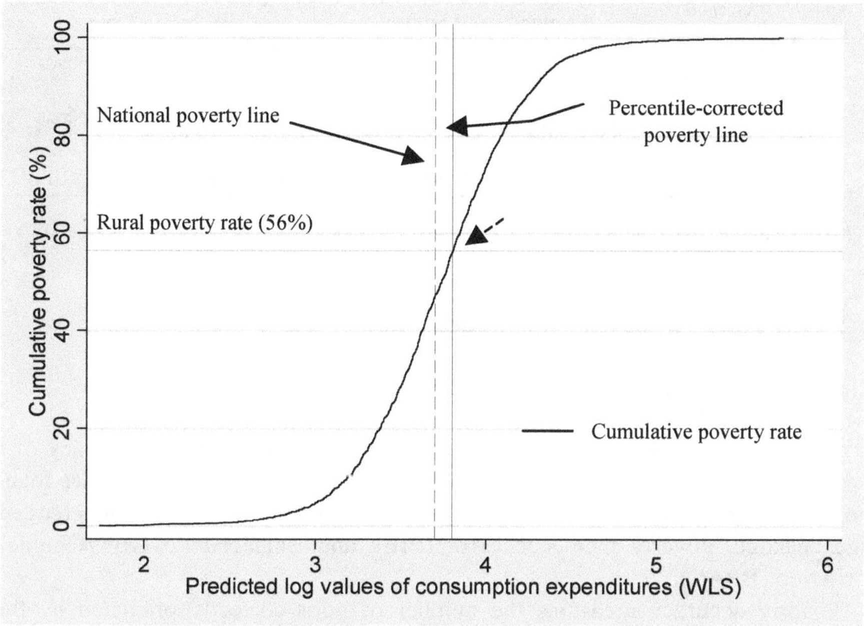

Source: Own results based on Malawi IHS2 data. The dashed arrow indicates the point at which the percentile-corrected poverty line crosses the distribution of poverty rate.

As shown in the graph, the PC poverty line determines the actual poverty rate in the distribution of predicted expenditures after calibrating the model. The graph also indicates that the difference between the national and PC poverty lines is minor.

The third approach used to classify households applied the cut-off that maximizes the Balanced Poverty Accuracy Criterion (BPAC), which is an overall performance measure of an estimation method[31]. Table 1 summarizes the decision rule for classifying households. The resulting classifications were crossed with the actual household poverty status to estimate the models' targeting performances as described in Section 2.3.

---

31 See Section 2.3 for further details on the BPAC.

Table 1. Decision rule for predicting household poverty status

Method Classification type	Weighted Least Square	Weighted Logit
Cut-off 1	Poverty line	Probability that corresponds to the poverty line
Cut-off 2	Percentile-corrected line (PC)	Probability that corresponds to the PC line
Cut-off 3	Poverty line that maximizes BPAC*	Probability that maximizes BPAC

Source: Own presentation. See Section 2.3 for details on BPAC.

2.3 Targeting ratios and robustness tests

2.3.1 Targeting ratios

Different ratios have been proposed in the literature to assess the accuracy of a poverty assessment model (see, for example, IRIS, 2005). In this paper, we focus on the most relevant ratios for targeting the poor: poverty accuracy, undercoverage, leakage, Poverty Incidence Error (PIE), and Balanced Poverty Accuracy Criterion (BPAC).

Poverty accuracy measures the number of poor correctly predicted by the method, expressed as a percentage of the total number of poor. Undercoverage and leakage are errors of predictions. While the former measures the number of poor incorrectly identified as non-poor, expressed as a percentage of the total number of poor, the latter estimates the number of non-poor who are wrongly identified as poor, expressed as a percentage of the total number of poor. Both ratios are widely used in the literature to assess the targeting efficiency of development policies (see, for example, Valdivia, 2005; Ahmed *et al.*, 2004; Weiss, 2004; and Ahmed and Bouis, 2002).

Poverty Incidence Error (PIE) indicates the precision of the model in correctly predicting the observed poverty rate. It is defined as the predicted poverty rate minus the actual rate, measured in percentage points. Ideally, the value of PIE should be zero, implying that the predicted poverty rate equals the observed poverty rate. Positive values of PIE indicate an overestimation of the poverty incidence, whereas negative values imply the opposite (van Bastelaer and Zeller, 2006). The Balanced Poverty Accuracy Criterion (BPAC), on the other hand, is used to assess a method's overall targeting performance. It is calculated as the poverty accuracy minus the absolute difference between undercoverage and leakage, measured in percentage points.

These three measures exhibit trade-offs. For example, minimizing leakage leads to higher undercoverage and lower poverty accuracy. Higher positive BPAC values indicate higher poverty accuracy, adjusted by the absolute difference between undercoverage and leakage. In the formulation of the BPAC, it is assumed that leakage and undercoverage are equally valued. Nevertheless, a policymaker may give higher or lower weight to undercoverage compared to leakage. This is, in principle, possible by altering the weight for leakage or undercoverage in the BPAC formula.

2.3.2 Model validations

A model with high predictive power in the validation sample is relevant for reaching most of the poor. Therefore, we performed out-of-sample validation tests to ascertain the predictive power and robustness of the models. The main purpose of the validation is to observe how well the models would perform in an independent sample derived from the same population. After estimation, the models were validated by applying the best set of indicators as well as their parameter estimates and identified cut-offs to the validation samples. Following the specifications in Section 2.2.2, for any household i in the validation samples, we predicted the consumption expenditures and probability of being poor as follows:

$$\hat{y}_i = \hat{\beta}_o + \hat{\beta}_1 x_{i1} + \hat{\beta}_o x_{i2} + \ldots + \hat{\beta}_k x_{ik} \qquad \textbf{(WLS)}$$

$$\hat{\rho}_i(z_i = 1 | x_i) = \frac{1}{1 + e^{-(\hat{\alpha}_o + \hat{\alpha}_1 x_{i1} + \hat{\alpha}_2 x_{i2} + \ldots + \hat{\alpha}_k x_{ik})}} \qquad \textbf{(WL)}$$

Furthermore, we assessed model robustness by estimating the prediction intervals using bootstrapped simulations. Bootstrap is a statistical procedure which models sampling from a population by the process of resampling from the sample (Hall, 1994). Approximate confidence intervals based on bootstrapped computations were introduced by Efron in 1979 (Efron, 1987; Horowitz, 2000). Unlike standard confidence interval estimation, bootstrap does not make any distributional assumption about the population and hence does not require the assumption of normality. Using the bootstrap approach, repeated random samples (resamples) of the same size as the validation samples were drawn with replacement. The set of best indicators, their parameter estimates, and their identified cut-offs were applied to each resample to predict the household poverty status and estimate the targeting ratios. These bootstrap estimates were then used to generate empirical distributions for the ratios.

Following Campbell and Torgerson (1999), we used 1,000 resamples from the validation sample for the estimations. For example, the rural validation sample of 3,280 households was repeatedly and randomly sampled (with replacement) to select 1,000 samples with 3,280 observations each. Under this sampling process, any household can be selected more than once in any given sample. Figure 2 illustrates the distribution of poverty accuracy from the 1,000 samples under the rural WLS model. This graph is superimposed with a normal curve. After generating the bootstrap distribution, the 2.5th and 97.5th percentiles were used as the limits for the interval at a 95% confidence level. Indeed, the graph shows that the estimated errors follow a normal distribution which justifies the selection of the predictions intervals.

Figure 2: Bootstrapped distribution of the poverty accuracy (rural WLS model).

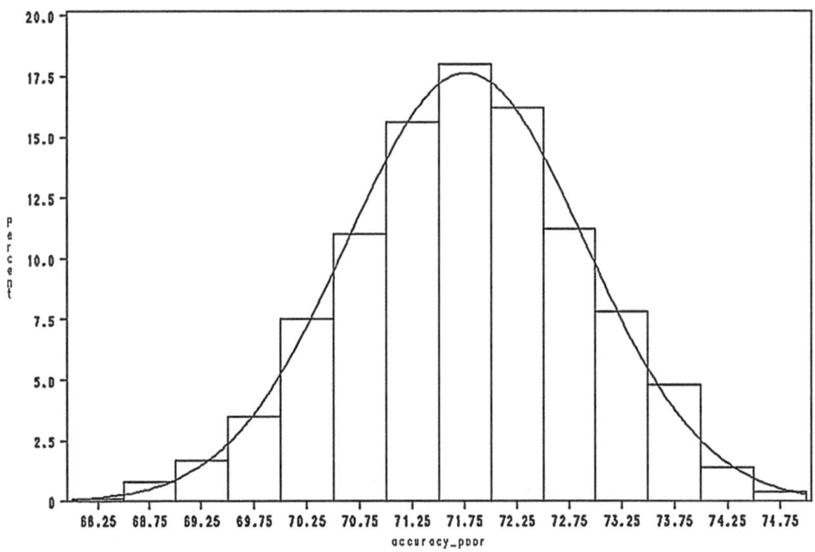

Source: Own results based on Malawi IHS2 data.

3. Results and discussions

This section discusses the results of the models out-of-sample[32]. First, we briefly describe the poverty lines which were applied and then we present the targeting performances of the models by regression method and poverty classification. The classification that yields the best performances is selected and flagged with the prediction intervals. Thereafter, we compare the aggregate accuracy of both estimation methods. Finally, we analyze the sensitivity of the models to the poverty line and examine the distribution of targeting errors.

3.1 Modelling the household poverty status: Empirical results

Table 2 gives an overview of the poverty lines and rates in Malawi. The full regression results, including the indicator lists are presented in Annex 2-5. Except for one, all of the parameter estimates are highly significant and their signs are consistent with expectations and economic theory.

Table 2. Malawi's poverty rates by rural/urban and poverty line (as of 2005)

Type of poverty line	Poverty lines (MK)	Poverty rate (in percent of people)		
		national	rural	urban
Extreme	29.81	26.21	28.66	8.72
National	44.29	52.40	56.19	25.23
International	59.18 (US $1.25 PPP)	69.52	73.59	40.26

Source: Own computations based on Malawi IHS2 data, Chen and Ravallion (2008), and World Bank (2008). MK denotes Malawi Kwacha, the Malawian currency. PPP stands for Purchasing Power Parity.

As shown in Table 2[33], the poverty rate in Malawi is estimated at 52.4% based on the national poverty line of MK44.29 or approximately US$0.40 (based on the 2005 official exchange rate). Although the poverty rate varies considerably be-

32 For brevity reasons, only out-of-sample results are presented throughout the paper. The results from the model calibrations are available upon request.

33 These rates differ slightly from official statistics because of errors in the weights of the IHS2 report.

tween urban and rural areas, this rate suggests that more than half of the population is unable to meet basic needs. Following Chen and Ravallion (2008), the international poverty line of US$1.25 a day was used. Converted to Malawi Kwacha (MK) using the 2005 Purchasing Power Parity (World Bank, 2008), the international poverty line is equivalent to MK59.18 a day. Under this line, the national poverty headcount is estimated at 69.52%. The extreme poverty line is defined as the line under which the poorest 50% of the population below the national poverty line live. This line is set at MK29.31. Under the extreme poverty line, 26% of the Malawian population are very poor. Table 3 presents the rural model's results by classification type.

Table 3. Rural model's predictive accuracy by classification type

Targeting ratios Method	Cut-off	Cut-off values*	Poverty accuracy (%)	Under-coverage (%)	Leakage (%)	PIE (% points)	BPAC (% points)
WLS	***National***	3.79	64.07	35.94	20.45	-7.32	48.58
	Percentile	3.80	65.43	34.58	21.74	-6.07	52.58
	MaxBPAC	3.85	72.00	28.00	26.32	-0.79	70.32
WL	***National***	0.59	58.77	41.23	16.58	-11.65	34.13
	Percentile	0.66	48.85	51.16	11.42	-18.78	9.10
	MaxBPAC	0.48	71.61	28.39	27.10	-0.61	70.32

Source: *Own computations based on Malawi IHS2 data. WLS denotes Weighted Least Square. WL denotes Weighted Logit. *Cut-off values are expressed as the logarithm of Malawi Kwacha (MK) for the WLS and as the probability of being poor for the WL. PIE denotes Poverty Incidence Error. BPAC denotes Balanced Poverty Accuracy Criterion.*

With regard to the WLS method, Table 3 suggests that the cut-off that maximizes the BPAC after calibrating the model (*MaxBPAC*) yields the best out-of-sample performances compared with the other two classification methods. This cut-off is followed by the percentile-corrected poverty line and the national poverty line. On the other hand, the *MaxBPAC* cut-off is associated with the highest leakage. The same trend applies to the WL method, except that the percentile-corrected poverty line yields the lowest performances under this method. The results show that classification by the *MaxBPAC* consistently yields the highest BPAC in the validation samples.

These results also illustrate the trade-off between undercoverage and leakage ratios; increasing the cut-off reduces undercoverage (improves the poverty accuracy), but also results in higher leakage to the non-poor[34]. Further results (not presented in this paper) suggest that the urban model follows the same pattern as the rural model. Therefore, we applied the cut-offs that maximize the BPAC after calibration to the validation samples. Table 4 summarizes the results, including the prediction intervals.

Table 4. Model predictive accuracy at optimal cut-offs

Targeting ratios Model	Method	Cut-off values*	Poverty accuracy (%)	Under-coverage (%)	Leakage (%)	PIE (% points)	BPAC (% points)
Rural	***WLS***	3.85	**72.00** (69.72; 74.22)	**28.00** (25.78; 30.28)	**26.32** (23.44; 29.14)	**-0.79** (-2.45; 0.96)	**70.32** (64.95; 73.49)
	WL	0.48	**71.61** (69.57; 74.02)	**28.39** (25.98; 30.43)	**27.10** (24.24; 29.95)	**-0.61** (-2.33; 1.13)	**70.32** (65.22; 73.23)
Urban	***WLS***	3.92	**62.16** (53.31; 70.98)	**37.84** (29.02; 46.69)	**38.74** (26.29; 52.85)	**0.21** (-3.54; 3.75)	**61.26** (40.90; 66.53)
	WL	0.39	**61.26** (51.67; 70.54)	**38.74** (29.46; 48.33)	**39.64** (27.34; 53.54)	**0.21** (-3.23; 3.96)	**60.36** (40.91; 66.03)

*Source: Own computations based on Malawi IHS2 data. Bootstrapped prediction intervals are in brackets. WLS denotes Weighted Least Square. WL denotes Weighted Logit. *Cut-off values are expressed as the logarithm of Malawi Kwacha (MK) under the WLS and as the probability of being poor under the WL. PIE denotes Poverty Incidence Error. BPAC denotes Balanced Poverty Accuracy Criterion.*

Table 4 indicates that under the WLS method, the rural model yields a poverty accuracy of 72% and a BPAC of 70.32 percentage points. This result suggests that the model is likely to cover about seven out of every ten poor households if applied to target the Malawian poor. The method's undercoverage is estimated at 28%, while its leakage is set at 26.32%. The PIE nears 0 percentage points, which implies that the method predicts the poverty rate out-of-sample almost perfectly. Likewise, the WL method yields a poverty accuracy of 71.61% and a BPAC of 70.32 percentage points when used to estimate the rural model. In addition, the method's estimated PIE is close to 0 percentage points, whereas its

34 When reducing the cut-off, this trade-off also applies to the WL method which estimates the probability of being poor.

undercoverage and leakage are estimated at 28.39% and 27.10%, respectively. These results show that under the rural model, the WLS and the WL yield the same BPAC and PIE, but the former slightly outperforms the latter in terms of poverty accuracy and leakage. Using the BPAC to assess the overall accuracy, the results show that both estimation methods perform the same under the rural model. Even when considering single targeting measures, such as poverty accuracy or leakage, there is not much difference between either method's targeting performance.

With regard to the urban model, Table 4 suggests that the WLS and WL methods yield the same PIE, estimated at 0.21 percentage points, which indicates that they both predict the poverty rate remarkably well. However, the former yields a slightly higher BPAC and poverty accuracy compared with the latter and also has lower leakage. These results show only small performance differences between both methods. Nonetheless, leakage and undercoverage rates are high under the urban model.

The relatively low performance of the urban model may be explained by the small calibration sample size, a less adapted set of indicators, and/or a low poverty rate in urban areas. This result may also be driven by the greater variability in consumption between different cities and households in urban areas. Estimates of the variances of household consumption expenditures confirm this argument[35]. Nevertheless, even though undercoverage and leakage rates are high in urban areas, these errors amount to relatively small numbers of poor; less than 15% of Malawians live in urban areas.

As concerns the prediction intervals, Table 4 indicates that their widths are very short under the rural model. For example, the estimated poverty accuracy under the rural WLS model has an interval width of 4.5 percentage points, whereas the BPAC has a width of 8.6 percentage points. These results imply that the model is very robust. Conversely, the performances of the urban model suggest a less robust tool with higher interval lengths.

As a whole, the above findings suggest that both estimation methods perform the same[36]. Furthermore, the rural model performs better than the urban model, which is less robust. Section 3.2 compares the aggregate performances of the estimation methods.

---

35 The variances were estimated at 0.70 for urban households versus 0.38 for rural households. For the four urban centers, they were set at 0.47, 0.95, 0.63, and 0.53 versus 0.34, 0.38, 0.26, 0.38, 0.38, 0.39, 0.38, and 0.35 for the eight agricultural development districts.

36 To allow for a stricter comparison of both estimation methods, we used the same indicator set to fit both regressions in separate simulations; however, the results do not differ from the observed performances.

3.2 Aggregate performances of the estimation methods

To compare the aggregate predictive power of the WLS and WL regressions, Receiver Operating Characteristic (ROC) curves were plotted based on the predictions of the validation samples. The ROC curve shows the trade-off between the coverage of the poor (i.e., poverty accuracy) and the inclusion of non-poor (i.e., inclusion error) at different cut-offs across the prediction spectra[37]. Earlier applications of ROC curves for poverty assessment include Wodon (1997), Baulch (2002), and Schreiner (2006) who applied the curve in combination with probit or logit regression in a calibration sample only. Apart from Houssou and Zeller (2010) and Johannsen (2009), no research has applied the ROC curve out-of-sample. Panel A of Figure 3 displays the ROC curves of the rural model.

Figure 3: ROC (A) and BPAC curves (B) of the rural model.

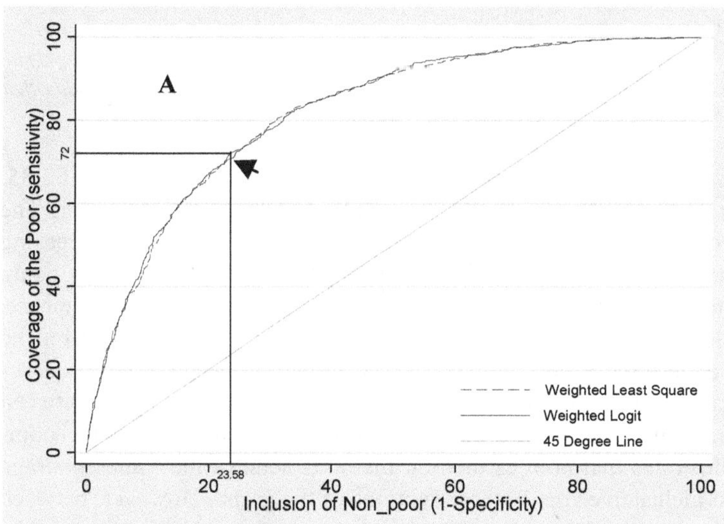

37 The coverage of the poor, or poverty accuracy, is also known as sensitivity. On the other hand, the inclusion of non-poor, or inclusion error is estimated as one minus specificity. It is the error of predicting non-poor as poor, expressed as a percentage of non-poor. It differs from leakage which is expressed as a percentage of the poor (see Wodon, 1997 and Baulch, 2002 for further details on ROC curves).

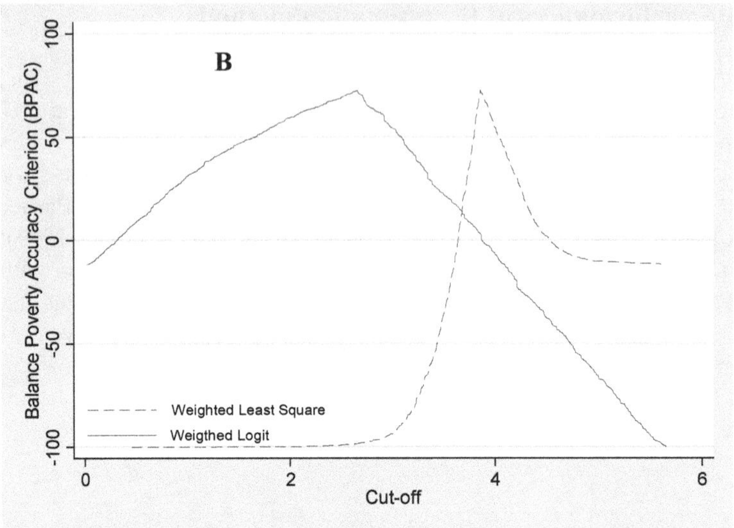

Source: Own results based on Malawi IHS2 data. The arrow on panel A indicates the point that matches the optimal cut-off value of 3.85 in Table 4.

Panel A shows that covering 72% of the poor (i.e., using a cut-off point of 3.85, as in Table 4) would lead to the inclusion of about 24% of the non-poor. The higher the coverage of the poor, the higher the inclusion of non-poor: increasing coverage to 90% would lead to more than 45% of non-poor households being wrongly targeted. Likewise, the curves follow a similar pattern with minor exceptions. While they both increase monotonically, their shape depends on the performances underlying each method used for targeting the poor. Both curves overlay perfectly in different sections of the graph: e.g., below 40%, between 50% and 65%, between 85% and 90%, and above 95% coverage of the poor. This pattern illustrates that both estimation methods achieve the same coverage of the poor and inclusion errors in these sections of the graph. However, between 40% and 50% coverage of the poor, WL slightly outperforms WLS, whereas the latter outperforms the former between 65% and 70% coverage of the poor. These results suggest that neither estimation method consistently yields the best performance across the entire ROC curves. Nevertheless, in the relevant band of sensitivity, from 70% to 90%, they perform nearly equally[38].

38 We consider the band [70% – 90%] as a good range for a reasonably accurate proxy means test model.

In panel B of Figure 3, we generate the BPAC curves for the entire cut-off spectra. These curves illustrate the BPAC distributions and their corresponding cut-offs in the rural validation sample. They show that the BPAC maxima (about 73 percentage points) differ only slightly from the performances presented in Table 4. This result is driven by the convergence of the cut-off optima between calibration and validation samples. In the validation sample, these cut-offs amount to 3.86 and 0.47 under the WLS and WL, respectively[39]. With respect to the urban model, the trends regarding the ROC and BPAC curves apply with minor exceptions (Figure 4). Within the relevant band of sensitivity, the WL outperforms the WLS in the lower section. The opposite is true in the upper section of the band.

Figure 4: ROC (C) and BPAC curves (D) of the urban model.

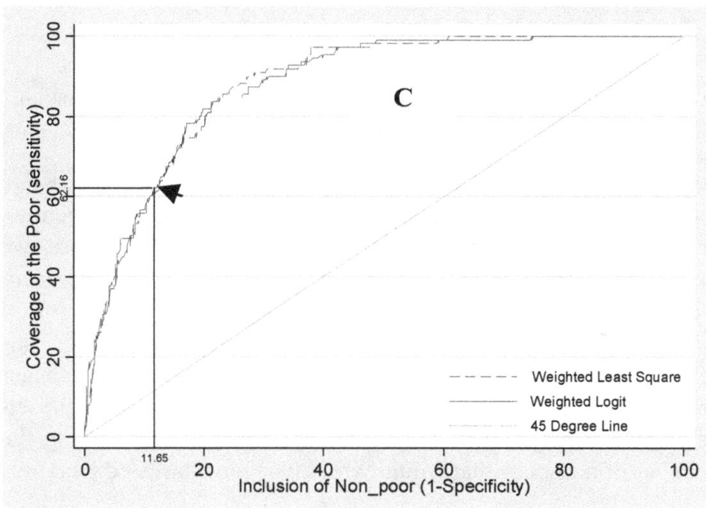

39 A similar trend emerges when the models were calibrated to the international and extreme poverty lines.

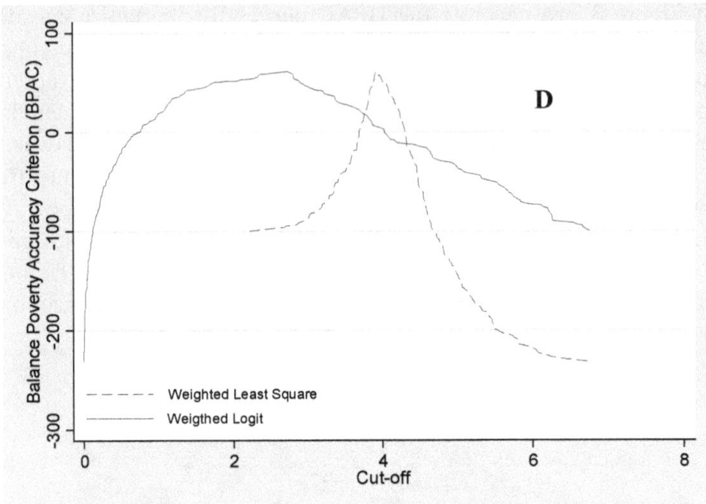

Source: Own results based on Malawi IHS2 data. The arrow on panel C indicates the point that matches the optimal cut-off value of 3.92 in Table 4.

On visual inspection, the areas under the ROC curves as well as their shapes are similar. A comparison reveals no statistically significant difference between the coverage of the poor from both curves under the same model. Therefore, we conclude that both estimation methods yield the same level of aggregate accuracy. The result is also consistent with the findings in Table 4.

As mentioned earlier, we used the cut-off that maximizes the BPAC for estimating targeting ratios. However, in practice a policymaker or program manager may use a different cut-off. In this regard, the ROC curve can guide them in setting the number of poor a program or project should reach and estimating the corresponding number of non-poor that would wrongly receive targeted benefits.

3.3 Assessing model sensitivity to the poverty line

Table 5 shows that raising the poverty line to US$1.25 (MK59.18) increases the BPAC and the coverage of the poor by about 10 percentage points to 14 percentage points depending on the model and estimation method, as well as reduces leakage by the same margin. These results indicate substantial improvements in the models' performances with about 82% and 74% of the poor correctly targeted under the rural and urban models, respectively. If such models are used for targeting, more than 70% of the poor would be covered.

Table 5. Model performance by poverty line

Targeting ratios Method/ Poverty line*		Cut-off values**	Poverty accuracy (%)	Under-coverage (%)	Leakage (%)	PIE (% points)	BPAC (% points)
			Rural Model				
WLS	*International*	4.03	**82.33** (80.86; 83.88)	**17.67** (16.13; 19.13)	**16.60** (14.71; 18.40)	**-0.70** (-2.26; 0.96)	**81.27** (77.72; 83.53)
WLS	*Extreme*	3.56	**49.93** (46.45; 53.41)	**50.07** (46.59; 53.55)	**39.21** (34.20; 44.46)	**-2.44** (-3.87; -0.98)	**39.08** (30.86; 48.09)
WL	*International*	0.56	**82.61** (81.14; 84.20)	**17.39** (15.80; 18.87)	**16.18** (14.40; 18.09)	**-0.79** (-2.22; 0.87)	**81.40** (77.91; 83.63)
WL	*Extreme*	0.36	**53.05** (49.61; 56.72)	**46.95** (43.28; 50.39)	**38.54** (33.51; 44.13)	**-1.89** (-3.37; -0.35)	**44.64** (35.95; 53.72)
			Urban Model				
WLS	*International*	4.18	**74.57** (68.30; 81.16)	**25.43** (18.85; 31.70)	**24.86** (17.39; 34.15)	**-0.21** (-3.75; 3.65)	**73.99** (59.50; 77.55)
WLS	*Extreme*	3.52	**50.00** (31.76; 67.74)	**50.00** (32.26; 68.24)	**73.53** (43.75; 123.44)	**1.67** (-0.83; 4.17)	**26.47** (-23.44; 50.51)
WL	*International*	0.43	**73.99** (67.66; 79.89)	**26.01** (20.11; 32.34)	**26.59** (18.57; 36.16)	**0.21** (-3.75; 3.96)	**73.41** (59.47; 76.57)
WL	*Extreme*	0.30	**47.06** (30.99; 64.71)	**52.94** (35.29; 69.01)	**61.77** (32.09; 104.45)	**0.63** (-1.88; 3.13)	**38.23** (-5.61; 51.72)

Source: *Own results based on Malawi IHS2 data. Bootstrapped prediction intervals are in brackets. WLS denotes Weighted Least Square. WL denotes Weighted Logit.*

* *See Table 2 for description of poverty lines.*

** *Cut-off values are expressed as the logarithm of Malawi Kwacha (MK) for the WLS and as the probability of being poor for the WL. PIE denotes Poverty Incidence Error. BPAC denotes Balanced Poverty Accuracy Criterion.*

Conversely, reducing the poverty line to MK29.31 drastically reduces the models' targeting performances. Under the rural model, the performances drop by 10 percentge points to 30 percentage points depending on the targeting ratios and estimation methods. Under the urban model, the reduction in performances ranges from 12 percentage points to 35 percentage points. These results indicate the difficulty of identifying the extremely poor by proxy means tests as overall error levels are high in this calibration.

Furthermore, both models estimate the observed poverty rates remarkably well when calibrated to the international poverty line. This is indicated by their estimated PIE values which are near 0 percentage points. The opposite pattern appears under the extreme poverty line. These results indicate that increasing the poverty line improves the models' targeting performances, whereas reducing the poverty line does the opposite. Therefore, it seems fair to say that the lower the poverty rate (ceteris paribus), the lower the models' performances and vice versa.

Likewise, the results show that both estimation methods do not differ much in terms of performances when calibrated to the international poverty line. The difference between both methods becomes more perceptible when the models were calibrated to the extreme poverty line. In separate simulations (not presented), the comparisons of the ROC curves point to the same conclusions. Section 3.4 analyzes the models' errors across consumption deciles.

3.4 Comparing model targeting errors across welfare deciles

The afore-mentioned results indicate that irrespective of the poverty line and model, the estimation methods yield some targeting errors. These errors are partly driven by inherent estimation errors. Although proxy means tests can improve the identification of the poor, they are not perfect.

The comparison of the estimation methods (Figure 5) suggests that they both follow the same pattern of errors across deciles under the same poverty line. Therefore, both methods do not differ in terms of targeting errors. More importantly, Figure 5 reveals that the rural model is progressive in targeting the poor: most of the poorest deciles are considerably covered, whereas most of the richest ones are excluded. Likewise, most of the poor whom the model fails to cover are the least poor. They are located just below the poverty line (e.g., at the 5th decile under the national poverty line). Similarly, most of those who are wrongly targeted are the least rich. They are concentrated just above the poverty line (rather than at the top of the distribution). The implication for targeting is that while there is bound to be some errors as no indicator is perfectly correlated with poverty, the models developed will accurately target most of the poorest deciles and will exclude most of the richest ones[40].

---

40 Further findings revealed the same pattern under the urban model. These results are available upon request.

Figure 5: Targeting errors by estimation method and poverty line (rural model).

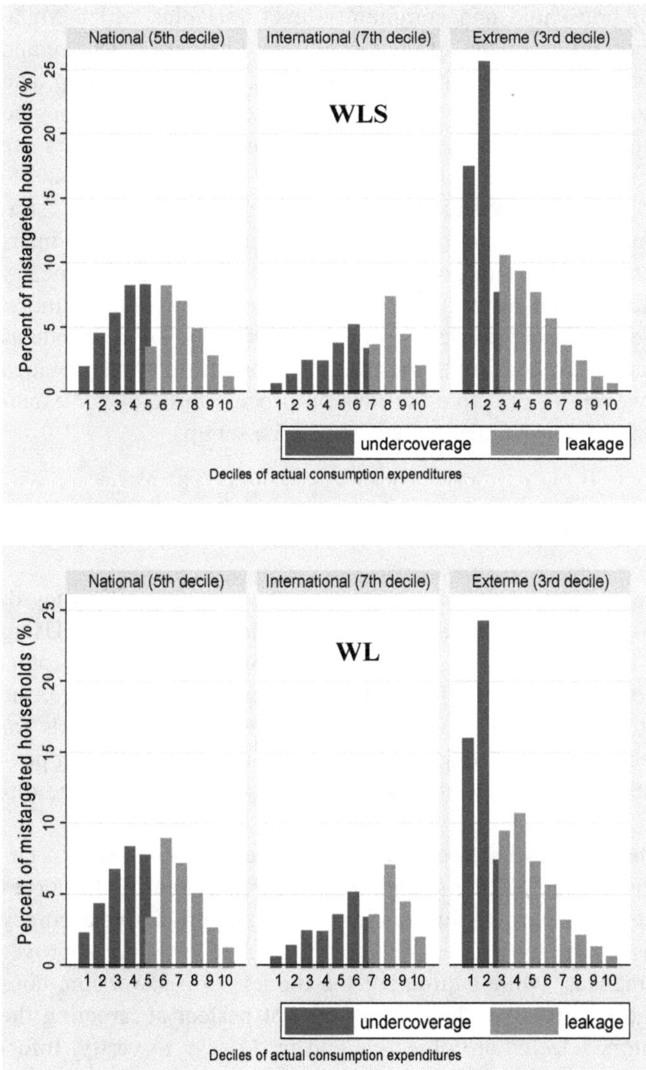

Source: Own results based on Malawi IHS2 data. WLS denotes Weighted Least Square. WL denotes Weighted Logit.

The sets of proxy indicators selected include variables from different dimensions of poverty, such as demography, education, housing, and assets. More importantly, they consist of household and community-level variables which Malawians perceive as important correlates of their welfare[41]. They are objective and fairly easy to verify (such as household size, floor material, bed ownership, and the number of household members who can read and write in English) as they do not include any monetary or subjective variables. While monetary indicators can be powerful poverty indicators (see, for example, Zeller and Alcaraz V., 2005; and Zeller *et al.*, 2005), they are hard to verify. Thus, such indicators allow strategic answers by respondents depending on their expectations from the interview. Likewise, with the lack of monetary transactions, estimations of monetary values (e.g., asset values) often result in imprecise measurements. Furthermore, the poverty proxies selected here are less prone to falsification by respondents and survey intermediaries. To confirm the accuracy of the information provided by the household, however, an effective verification process through, for example, random household visits, triangulation, etc. should be set up.

4. Concluding remarks

This paper develops empirical models for improving the targeting efficiency of development policies which rely on targeting household-level poverty. Using household-level data from Malawi, this paper focuses on improving indicator-based models that identify poor households more accurately. Furthermore, the paper analyzes the out-of-sample performances of two estimation methods for targeting the poor. Because a set of policies might explicitly target different poverty groups in the population, the developed models are calibrated to three different poverty lines.

Findings suggest that both estimation methods achieve the same level of targeting performances out-of-sample. This result is confirmed by their ROC curves which indicate that there is no sizable difference in aggregate predictive accuracy between both methods. Calibrating the models to a higher poverty line improves their targeting performances, while calibrating the models to a lower line does the opposite. Although progressive, the models are not perfect at targeting the poor. The best indicators selected are objective and fairly easy to verify. Information on these indicators can be easily and quickly elicited.

The models developed here offer a better prospect for improving the poverty outreach of development policies in Malawi. Such operational models can also

41 See Benson *et al.* (2006) for a study on the perceptions of welfare by Malawian households.

be useful for assessing whether a project, policy, or development institution reaches the poor. Nevertheless, the observed patterns could be refined with additional validations across time. This research can be extended to other countries, especially to those with high levels of poverty.

References

Ahmed, A., Rashid, S., Sharma, M., and Zohir, S. (2004) Food Aid Distribution in Bangladesh: Leakage and Operational Performance. Discussion Paper No. 173. Washington, D.C.: The International Food Policy Research Institute.

Ahmed, A. and Bouis, H. E. (2002) Weighting what's practical: Proxy means tests for targeting food subsidies in Egypt. *Food Policy* 27: 519-540.

Baulch, B. (2002) Poverty Monitoring and Targeting Using ROC Curves: Examples from Vietnam. Working Paper No. 161. University of Sussex: The Institute of Development Studies.

Benson, T. Payongayong, E., Ahmed A., and Sharma M. (2006) Towards Operational Methods in Measuring Absolute Income Poverty. Paper presented at the 26th International Association of Agricultural Economists conference; 16-18 August, Gold Coast, Australia.

Benson, T. (2002) Malawi – An Atlas of Social Statistics. National Statistics Office and International Food Policy Research Institute, Washington DC.

Besley, T. and Kanbur, R. (1993) The Principles of Targeting. In: Lipton, M. and J. Van Der Gaag, (eds) *Including the Poor.* Proceedings of a Symposium Organized by the World Bank and the International Food Policy Research Institute; December, Washington D.C.: The World Bank, pp. 67-90.

Braithwaite, J. Grootaert, C., and Milanovic, B. (2000) *Poverty and Social Assistance in Transition Countries.* New York: Saint Martin's Press.

Campbell, M.K. and Torgerson, D. J. (1999) Bootstrapping: Estimating confidence intervals for cost-effectiveness ratios. *International Journal of Medicine* 92 (3): 177-182.

Chen, S. and Ravallion, M. (2008) The Developing World is Poorer than we Thought, but no less Successful in the Fight Against Poverty. Policy Research Working Paper No. 4703. Washington D.C.: The World Bank.

Chinsinga, B. (2005) The Clash of voices: Community-based targeting of safety-net interventions in Malawi. *Social Policy and Administration* 39 (3): 284-301.

Coady, D. and Parker, S. (2009) Targeting performance under self-selection and administrative targeting methods. *Economic Development and Cultural Change* 57 (3): 559-587.

Coady, D., Grosh, M., and Hodinott, J. (2002) The Targeting of Transfer in Developing Countries: Review of Experiences and Lessons. Washington D.C.: The World Bank.

Deaton, A. (1997) *The Analysis of Household Surveys: A Microeconometric Approach to Development Policy.* Washington D.C.: Johns Hopkins University Press.

Efron, B. (1987) Better bootstrap confidence intervals. *Journal of the American Statistical Association* 82 (397): 171-185.

Glewwe, P. (1992) Targeting assistance to the poor: Efficient allocation of transfers when household income is not observed. *Journal of Development Economics* 38 (2): 297-321.

Government of Malawi and World Bank (2007) Malawi Poverty and Vulnerability Assessment: Investing into our Future, Synthesis Report. Malawi.

Greene, W. H. (2003) *Econometric Analysis.* Fifth Edition, Pearson Education Inc. New Jersey: Prentice Hall.

Grootaert, C. and Braithwaite, J. (1998) Poverty Correlates and Indicator-based Targeting in Eastern Europe and the Former Soviet Union. Washington D.C.: The World Bank.

Grosh, M. E. and Baker, J. L. (1995) Proxy Means Tests for Targeting Social Programs: Simulations and Speculation. Working Paper No. 118. Washington D.C.: The World Bank.

Gujarati, D. (2006) *Essentials of Econometrics.* International Edition, New York: McGraw Hill.

Hall, P. (1994) Methodology and Theory for the Bootstrap. In: R. F. Engle and D. L. McFadden (eds) *Handbook of Econometrics* IV, Elsevier Science B. V., pp. 2342-2379.

Hentschel, J., Lanjouw, J.O., Lanjouw, P., and Poggi, J. (2000) Combining census and survey data to trace the spatial dimensions of poverty: A case study of Ecuador. *World Bank Economic Review* 14 (1): 1471-165.

Horowitz, J. (2000) The Bootstrap. University of Iowa: The Department of Economics.

Houssou N. and Zeller M. (2010) Targeting the poor and smallholder farmers: Empirical evidence from Malawi. *Quarterly Journal of International Agriculture* 49 (4): 341-358.

IRIS. (2005) Note on Assessment and Improvement of Tool Accuracy. Mimeograph, University of Maryland: The IRIS Center.

Johannsen, J. (2009) *Operational Assessment of Monetary Poverty by Proxy Means Tests: The Example of Peru.* F. Heidhues, J. von Braun, and M. Zeller (eds) *Development Economics and Policy 65*, Frankfurt: Peter Lang.

Levy, S. and Barahona, C. (2002) Targeted Inputs Programme (TIP): Main Report of the

Evaluation Programme. Report submitted to the Ministry of Agriculture and Irrigation (Malawi) and the Department for International Development, UK.

National Statistics Office (2005) Malawi Second Integrated Household Survey (IHS2): Basic Information Document. Zomba, Malawi.

Poverty Monitoring System (2000) The State of Malawi's Poor: The Incidence, Depth, and Severity of Poverty. Policy. Brief No.2, Malawi.

Ravallion, M. and Chao, K. (1989) Targeted policies for poverty alleviation under imperfect information: Algorithms and applications. *Journal of Policy Modelling* 11 (2): 213-224.

SAS Institute (2003) The Logistic procedure: Effect Selection Methods. Cary, NC.

Schreiner, M. (2006) A Simple Poverty Scorecard for India. Microfinance Risk Management, Washington University in Saint Louis: The Center for Social Development.

United Nations (2009) Millennium Development Goals Report. New York: The United Nations.

Valdivia, M. (2005) Is Identifying the Poor the Main Problem in Targeting Nutritional Program? Discussion Paper No. 7. Washington D.C.: The World Bank.

van Bastelaer, T. and Zeller M. (2006) *Achieving the Microcredit Summit and Millennium Development Goals of Reducing Extreme Poverty: What is the Cutting Edge on Cost-effectively Measuring Movement Across the $1/Day Threshold?* S. Daley-Harris and A. Awimbo (eds) *More Pathways out of Poverty*. Kumarian Press, Inc., pp. 1-41.

Weiss, J. (2004) Reaching the Poor with Poverty Projects: What is the Evidence on Social Returns? Research Paper No. 61. Tokyo: The Asian Development Bank Institute.

Wodon, Q. (1997) Targeting the poor using ROC curves. *World Development* 25 (12): 2083-2092.

Wooldridge, J. M. (2006) *Introductory Econometrics: A Modern Approach*. Third Edition, Ohio: Thomson South-Western.

World Bank (2009) Malawi – Country Brief. www.worldbank.org. (Accessed September 11, 2009).

– (2008) Global Purchasing Power Parities and Real Expenditures 2005 International Comparison Program (ICP) Washington D.C.: The World Bank.

– (2007) Malawi Social Protection Status Report No. 40027-MW. Sustainable Development Network, Africa Region. Washington D.C.: The World Bank.

Zeller, M., Sharma, M., Henry, C., and Lapenu, C. (2006) An operational tool for assessing the poverty outreach performance of development policies and projects: Results of case studies in Africa, Asia, and Latin America. *World Development* 34 (3): 446-464.
Zeller, M. and Alcaraz V., G. (2005) Developing and Testing Poverty Assessment Tools: Results from Accuracy Tests in Uganda. University of Maryland College Park: The IRIS Center.
Zeller, M., Alcaraz V., G., and Johannsen, J. (2005) Developing and Testing Poverty Assessment Tools: Results from Accuracy Tests in Bangladesh. University of Maryland College Park: The IRIS Center.

Annexes

Annex 1. Sample size by model type

Sub-samples	Rural model	Urban model	Total
Total sample size	9,840	1,440	11,280
- calibration (2/3)	6,560	960	7,540
- validation (1/3)	3,280	480	3,760
Number of indicators	148	112	-

Source: Own results based on Malawi IHS2 data.

Annex 2. Weighted Least Square estimates (rural model)

Model significance F: 329.25***

Adj. R^2: 0.46 — Number of observations: 6,560

Dependent variable:
Logarithm of household daily per capita expenditures in Malawi Kwacha

	Indicator set	Parameter Estimates	Robust Standard Errors	T-values
	Intercept	4.34***	0.04	117.10
Control variables	Agricultural development district Mzuzu	0.08**	0.03	2.27
	Agricultural development district Kasungu	0.26***	0.03	8.02
	Agricultural development district Salima	0.16***	0.04	4.47
	Agricultural development district Lilongwe	0.22***	0.03	6.92
	Agricultural development district Machinga	-0.08**	0.03	-2.49
	Agricultural development district Blantyre	-0.04	0.03	-1.14
	Agricultural development district Ngabu	0.01	0.04	0.27
Best 10 indicators	1. Household size	-0.17***	0.00	-51.20
	2. Number of members who can read English	0.08***	0.01	13.56
	3. Household grew tobacco in the past five cropping seasons	0.12***	0.02	7.28
	4. Floor of main dwelling is predominantly made of smooth cement	0.19***	0.02	9.66
	5. Number of separate rooms occupied by household, excluding toilet, storeroom, or garage	0.05***	0.01	8.58
	6. Cooking fuel is collected firewood	-0.15***	0.02	-8.37
	7. Bed ownership	0.16***	0.02	9.85
	8. Tape, CD player, or HiFi stereo ownership	0.18***	0.02	9.37
	9. Electric, gas stove, or hot plate ownership	0.61***	0.08	7.43
	10. Bicycle ownership	0.15***	0.01	11.88

Source: Own results based on Malawi IHS2 data.
*** *denotes significant at the 99% level.*
** *denotes significant at the 95% level. CD denotes Compact Disk. HiFi denotes High Fidelity.*

Annex 3. Weighted Logit estimates (rural model)

Likelihood ratio: 877042.54*** Wald Statistic: 520598.86***
Score: 721528.13*** Number of observations: 6,560

Dependent variable:
Logarithm of household daily per capita expenditures in Malawi Kwacha

	Indicator set	Parameter Estimates	Robust Standard Errors	Wald Chi-Square
Control variables	Intercept	-1.50***	0.18	22891.54
	Agricultural development district Mzuzu	-0.48***	0.19	1972.80
	Agricultural development district Kasungu	-1.26***	0.19	13756.95
	Agricultural development district Salima	-0.33***	0.02	887.51
	Agricultural development district Lilongwe	-0.97***	0.17	9748.01
	Agricultural development district Machinga	0.29***	0.17	914.53
	Agricultural development district Blantyre	0.03***	0.17	9.97
	Agricultural development district Ngabu	-0.07***	0.20	35.86
Best 10 indicators	1. Household size	0.70***	0.02	421164.02
	2. Number of male adults in the household	-0.28***	0.05	11877.87
	3. Number of members who can read Eng-lish	-0.30***	0.03	29751.16
	4. Household grew tobacco in past five cropping seasons	-0.48***	0.10	11686.45
	5. Floor of main dwelling is predominantly made of smooth cement	-0.97***	0.12	29707.05
	6. If any household member (s) sleeps un der a bed net	-0.45***	0.07	14831.05
	7. Bed ownership	-0.56***	0.09	15565.33
	8. Tape, CD player, or HiFi ownership	-0.71***	0.12	15968.65
	9. Bicycle ownership	-0.48***	0.07	17194.07
	10. Paraffin lantern ownership	-0.49***	0.08	15156.78

Source: Own results based on Malawi IHS2 data.
*** *denotes significant at the 99% level.*
** *denotes significant at the 95% level. CD denotes Compact Disk. HiFi denotes High Fidelity.*

Annex 4. Weighted Least Square estimates (urban model)

	Model significance F: 176.05***			
Adj. $\mathbf{R^2}$: 0.70		Number of observations: 960		
	Dependent variable: **Logarithm of household daily per capita expenditures in Malawi Kwacha**			
	Indicator set	Parameter Estimates	Robust Standard Errors	T-values
Control variables	Intercept	4.90***	0.06	77.02
	Lilongwe city	0.06	0.05	1.22
	Zomba city	-0.35***	0.06	-6.16
	Blantyre city	-0.20***	0.05	-4.03
Best 10 indicators	1. Household size	-0.24***	0.01	-24.46
	2. Number of members who can read English	0.07***	0.01	5.72
	3. Maximum class level ever attended in the household is superior or post-secondary	0.41***	0.08	4.92
	4. Number of separate rooms occupied by Household, excluding toilet, storeroom, or garage	0.08***	0.02	4.64
	5. Cooking fuel is collected firewood	-0.42***	0.05	-7.93
	6. Household owns a landline telephone in working condition	0.35***	0.08	4.12
	7. Household has working electricity in the house	0.32***	0.05	6.49
	8. Bed ownership	0.26***	0.04	6.63
	9. Television & VCR ownership	0.33***	0.07	4.62
	10. Electric, gas stove, or hot plate ownership	0.26***	0.08	3.29

Source: Own results based on Malawi IHS2 data.
*** *denotes significant at the 99% level.*
** *denotes significant at the 95% level.* VCR denotes Video Cassette Recorder.

Annex 5. Weighted Logit estimates (urban model)

Likelihood ratio: 140465.17***	Wald Statistic: 63111.55***
Score: 123575.76 ***	Number of observations: 960

	Dependent variable: **Logarithm of household daily per capita expenditures in Malawi Kwacha**			
	Indicator set	Parameter Estimates	Robust Standard Errors	Wald Chi-Square
	Intercept	-3.91***	0.61	12181.58
Control variables	Lilongwe city	0.04	0.35	2.39
	Zomba city	1.01***	0.39	1168.71
	Blantyre city	0.99***	0.38	1704.27
Best 10 indicators	1. Household size	0.72***	0.07	40401.76
	2. Number of members who can read English	-0.12***	0.11	636.19
	3. Household can read Chichewa language	-0.67***	0.28	2114.77
	4. Highest class level ever attended by females in the household is secondary or post primary	-1.47***	0.43	5294.98
	5. Dwelling construction material is traditional	0.86***	0.27	3499.26
	6. Cooking fuel is collected firewood	0.93***	0.33	2905.11
	7. Household has working electricity in the house	-1.75***	0.60	5094.95
	8. Household head sleeps on a mat (grass) on the floor	1.02***	0.27	5903.42
	9. Television & VCR ownership	-2.11***	0.71	1984.65
	10. If there is a place to purchase common medicines, such as a panadol, in the community	-0.83***	0.38	1697.95

Source: Own results based on Malawi IHS2 data.
*** *denotes significant at the 99% level.*
** *denotes significant at the 95% level.* VCR denotes Video Cassette Recorder.

Chapter IV: To Target or Not to Target? The costs, benefits, and impacts of indicator-based targeting[42]

Abstract

This paper assesses the cost-effectiveness of indicator-based targeting. Using household survey data from Malawi, we examine whether an indicator-based system is more target and cost-efficient in reaching the poor than universal systems and the currently used mechanisms for targeting agricultural subsidies in the country.

Estimation results suggest that targeting Malawi's poor and smallholder farmers with indicator-based systems may be worth the extra effort and may improve program targeting and cost efficiency. Even though under the proposed system administrative costs increase, simulation results indicate that it does not make a targeted program cost-ineffective. More importantly, the proposed system appears to be more target and cost-efficient than the 2000/01 Targeted Input Program (TIP) and the 2006/07 Agricultural Input Support Program (AISP), both of which were administered through community-based targeting systems. While TIP and AISP transferred about 50% of total transfer, under the proposed system, about 73% of transfers are delivered to the poor and smallholder farmers. Additionally, the costs of leakage to the non-poor are cut by more than 50% under the proposed system.

We conclude from the above findings that the newly proposed system can potentially improve the targeting and cost efficiency of Malawi's development programs. However, such improvements depend on actual implementation of targeted programs, a critical issue that should not be set aside.

Keywords: Malawi, poverty targeting, out-of-sample tests, redistribution, cost-effectiveness, agricultural subsidy.

1. Introduction

As governments and the donor community face the pressing need to meet the Millennium Development Goals (MDGs) and end poverty, the provision of targeted programs (e.g. free/subsidized inputs, food, cash-for-work, health care, education, etc.) has become essential to development policy in many poor countries. This is also the case for Malawi where 52.4% of the population are poor (National Statistics Office – NSO, 2005a).

---

42 This article has been reprinted from Nazaire Houssou and Manfred Zeller (2011): To Target or not Target? The costs, benefits and impacts of indicator-based targeting. *Food Policy*, Volume 36 (5) pp.: 627–637, reproduced with permission from Elsevier Ltd.

In response to endemic poverty, poor harvest, severe food insecurity, and unfavorable weather conditions, Malawi's decision makers have devised successive development programs, such as the Universal Starter Pack, the Targeted Input Program (TIP) and the Agricultural Input Support Programs (AISPs) which targeted the poor and smallholder farmers. The issue of fertilizer subsidies is right at the top of the political agenda in Malawi and its example is being widely touted as the African Green Revolution. However, such a policy has proven controversial in recent years (see, for example, Harrigan, 2008). Preliminary assessments of the AISPs suggest that the programs have improved household food security and led to an increase of the country's national maize output with some of parts of the production being exported to neighboring countries (Dorward et al., 2008; Minde et al., 2008).

Input subsidy and other development programs rely mostly on community-based targeting mechanisms in which local authorities and other community representatives select program beneficiaries based on their assessment of household living standards. However, most of these programs display a poor targeting performance (in terms of the proportion of poor who receive program benefits and the proportion of non-poor who are wrongly targeted) due to a number of factors, including various local perceptions, favoritism, loosely defined or misunderstood targeting criteria, political interests, implementation problems, among others. According to the Malawi Second Integrated Household Survey (IHS2), about 35% of the rural poor did not receive TIP, while 62% of the rural non-poor did benefit from the program. Likewise, an evaluation of the 2006/2007 AISP program by Dorward et al. (2008) suggests that 46% of the poor did not receive fertilizer vouchers, whereas 54% of the non-poor were wrongly targeted. Furthermore, a study by Ricker-Gilbert and Jayne (2009) suggests that the 2006/2007 AISP was targeted at wealthier and politically well-connected farmers who would otherwise have purchased the fertilizer, causing substantial displacement estimated at about 30% to 40% on the market (Dorward et al., 2008). Hence, most development observers agree that much more needs to be done to improve the country's targeting mechanisms. The need to control costs and ensure that fertilizer subsidies reach their intended beneficiaries is essential in a high cost importing and poor country, such as Malawi.

Therefore, this research explores whether an indicator-based system can improve the targeting of the poor and smallholder farmers in the country. Furthermore, the study assesses whether such a system is more target- and cost-efficient than universal interventions and the targeting mechanisms currently in use in Malawi. Findings suggest that indicator-based targeting of the poor might be an alternative for improving the targeting efficiency of the country's development programs. This paper is organized as follows: Section 2 discusses the targeting of development programs within the context of Malawi, Section 3 briefly reviews the principles of targeting, Section 4 describes the methodology, Section 5 presents the results, and Section 6 ends the work with some concluding remarks.

2. Targeted development programs: The Malawian context

Malawi is mostly an agricultural country with more than 80% of its population living in rural areas and about 90% of its households working in the agricultural sector. In 2007, the agricultural sector contributed about 34% to the Gross Domestic Product (GDP) (World Bank, 2009a) and accounted for more than 80% of export earnings (World Bank, 2009b). Widespread poverty is a major obstacle to the country's economic growth and development.

Historically, there has been no coherent strategy for targeting the poor and vulnerable in Malawi (Smith, 2001). A large number of targeted programs exist, most of which are uncoordinated short-term relief or emergency responses. In the period from 2003 to 2006, the combined safety nets/social protection system, including emergency aid and disaster response, amounted to an average of more than US$134 million per year, that is about 6.5% of the country's GDP (World Bank, 2007).

Fertilizer subsidy is a key element of the Malawian government's present policy (World Bank, 2007). The provision of agricultural inputs, especially fertilizer, enjoys a special place in the popular hierarchy of anti-poverty and food policy measures in Malawi (Smith, 2001). For example, the Universal Starter Pack of 1998/99 provided ten kilograms (kg) of fertilizer, along with seeds, to all smallholder households at a cost of US$27 million. But, confronted with the fiscal burden and donor pressure[43], the government subsequently scaled down the program to a targeted version in 2000/2001, which is also known as the Targeting Input Program (TIP).

Following an extremely poor harvest in 2004/2005, a new fertilizer subsidy program was devised in the country in the 2005/2006 growing season. The program was scaled up in the following year. The 2006/2007 AISP program provided fertilizer and seeds to just under 2.8 million households and cost about US$91 million (Dorward et al., 2008). The program distributes about 3.48 million fertilizer coupons which entitle each qualified farming household to purchase one 50kg bag of urea and one 50kg bag of NPK (Nitrogen, Phosphorus, and Potassium) at a subsidized rate of MK950, or approximately 28% of market price.

43 See Harrigan (2008).

Most of these previous programs were implemented through community-based targeting mechanisms (see Chinsinga, 2005a, b; Levy and Barahona, 2002; Conning and Kevanne, 2002 for further details on community-based targeting systems). However, they are poorly targeted at their intended beneficiaries because targeting criteria are loosely defined and leave major judgments to the communities who often argue that "they are all poor." Almost all development interventions have targeting problems in the country (Government of Malawi, -GoM and World Bank, 2007); they cover a limited number of poor and leak program benefits to a significant number of non-poor. To put this in perspective, we estimate the targeting efficiency of selected programs as measured by their undercoverage and leakage rates (Table 1).

Table 1. Targeting efficiency of Malawi's development programs

Program type	Undercoverage (%)	Leakage (%)
Free food distribution	70.99	31.23
Input-for-work	98.61	0
TIP (rainy season)[a]	34.98	61.81
TIP (dry season)[a]	94.96	8.03
Food/cash-for-work	93.06	6.19
ILTPWP	72.9	2.6
AISP	46	54
Average performance	*73.07*	*23.41*

Note: *Undercoverage is defined as the number of poor who did not receive program benefits, whereas leakage is the number of non-poor households who receive program benefits. Both measures are expressed as a percentage of the total number of poor. AISP denotes Agricultural Input Support Program. The Improved Livelihood Through Public Works Programs (ILTPWP) was implemented in six districts of the central region of Malawi. [a]Results based on rural areas estimates only.*

Source: *Own results based on Malawi IHS2 data plus excerpts from World Bank (2006) and estimates based on Dorward et al. (2008).*

Table 1 suggests that Malawi's development programs are badly targeted, with average undercoverage and leakage rates estimated at about 73% and 23%, respectively. The results are consistent with the World Bank's (2007) which show that the level of funding for different programs in the country is not necessarily inadequate, but that many programs suffer from limited beneficiary coverage, mis-targeting, and significant leakages to the non-poor. Additionally, most of them are too small in scale to have a meaningful impact.

Though program beneficiaries were presumed to be selected based on multiple indicators, poverty has always been a major targeting criterion in previous programs (see Dorward et al., 2008; Chinsinga 2005a, b; Lawson et al., 2002; Levy and Barahona, 2002). Furthermore, Dorward et al. (2008) indicate that fertilizer subsidies were allocated to wealthier farmers (causing substantial displacement), whereas Ricker-Gilbert and Jayne (2009) emphasize that those subsidies should be given to the poor who, based on the IHS2 data, hold as much land as the non-poor.[44]

Clearly, under the current community-based targeting system, Malawi's development programs are not reaching many of the poor and smallholder farmers. To reverse this trend, we propose targeting by proxy means tests[45] which offers a better prospect for improving the targeting efficiency of the country's development programs.

3. The principles of targeting: A theoretical perspective

The principles of targeting are well established in the literature[46]. However, less is known about the costs of targeting. By definition, targeting is the process by which benefits are channelled to the members of the high priority group that a program aims to serve (Grosh and Baker, 1995). The case for narrow targeting rests on the existence of a budget constraint (Coady et al., 2004). Targeting involves two elements: first, defining who should receive benefits (e.g. the poor, the vulnerable, or food insecure households) and second, establishing mechanisms for identifying those people[47].

However, targeting is not costless. It imposes administrative costs that reduce the amount of benefits available for the actual intervention (Hoddinott, 1999). To our knowledge, no feasible targeting mechanism is perfect; all available options involve two types of errors: undercoverage and leakage. Undercoverage, or error of exclusion, is the failure of a program to cover all of its intended beneficiaries[48]. Leakage, or error of inclusion, is the error of including non-poor as program beneficiaries. While effective targeting may reduce the government's direct

44 Our estimates based on the IHS2 indicate that there is no statistically significant difference in agricultural landholding between Malawian poor and non-poor.

45 See Section 4 for further details on proxy means tests.

46 See Besley and Kanbur (1993) for further details on the principles of targeting.

47 See below for a brief survey of these mechanisms.

48 Intended program beneficiaries need not necessarily be the poor.

costs for providing benefits, it does not necessarily reduce the total costs of a targeted program (Rook and Freeland, 2006; Dutrey, 2007).

Targeting entails a number of costs. These include the costs of transfer to the poor, the costs of leakage to the non-poor, administrative costs, and the hidden costs of targeting which comprise: private costs, indirect costs, social, and political costs[49]. Administrative costs include the costs of developing a targeting algorithm (e.g. developing a proxy means test model), the costs of regular screening of program beneficiaries, the costs of processing and delivering program benefits, and program staff costs. It is generally agreed that the finer the targeting, the higher the costs of administration and the greater the hidden costs. Figure 1 shows the administrative and hidden costs of targeting as a function of the coverage of the population.

Figure 1: Costs of targeting.

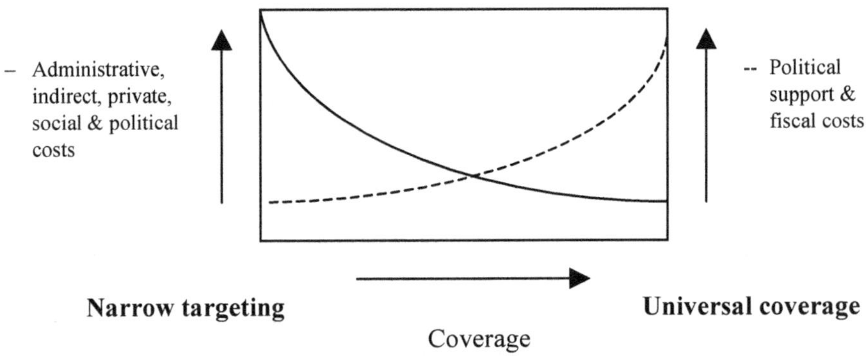

Source: Adapted from Smith (2001).

Figure 1 suggests that narrow targeting (of the poor) increases administrative, indirect, private, social, and political costs and reduces fiscal costs. As the coverage of the population increases towards universal regime, the administrative, indirect, private, social, and political costs fall, whereas political support improves (i.e. political costs fall) and fiscal costs increase due to excessive leakage to the non-poor. Though either a universal regime or a completely narrow targeting

49 See Rook and Freeland (2006); Coady et al., (2002), and van de Walle (1998) for a fuller description of targeting costs and benefits.

would cover all of the poor, these schemes would be extremely costly and unaffordable to most developing countries, including Malawi[50].

The alternative is to consider an intermediate solution which lies somewhere in the middle of the curves (Smith, 2001). The intermediate solution consists of targeting through various methods, including indicator-based targeting methods (e.g. proxy means targeting, categorical targeting), geographical targeting, community-based targeting, self-targeting, and subjective self-assessment[51]. All of these targeting methods have the same goal: to correctly and efficiently identify which households are poor and which are not. However, none of them is perfect at targeting poverty. Most often, they exhibit a trade-off between accuracy (measured by the proportion of poor and non-poor covered) and practicality/costs of implementation as shown in Figure 2.

Figure 2: Trade-off between practicality and accuracy

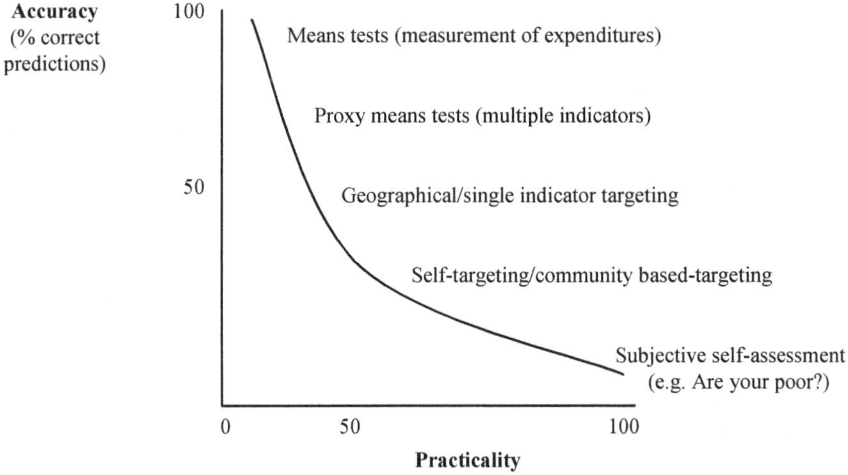

Source: Own conception.

Figure 2 shows that the higher the method's accuracy, the lower the practicality (i.e. the higher the costs of implementation) and vice versa. Compared with most targeting methods on the graph, proxy means tests have the merit of making rep-

50 A completely narrow targeting implies the identification of the poor through a verified means test which is based on direct measurements of household expenditures or income in the total population.

51 See Coady et al., (2002); Conning and Kevane (2002); and Grosh and Baker (1995) for a fuller description of targeting methods.

licable judgments using consistent and visible criteria (Coady et al., 2002). They are also quick, easy to implement, and less costly than sophisticated means tests which require a regular collection of data on household expenditures or income. In a recent review of 122 targeted anti-poverty interventions, Coady et al. (2004) found that proxy means tests show good results on average, even though there is a wide variation in targeting performance between programs.

Furthermore, Coady and Parker (2009) indicate that administrative selection based on proxy means testing is particularly effective at reducing overall program coverage while maintaining high coverage of the lowest welfare households. Therefore, we propose targeting the poor and smallholder farmers by proxy means tests. Proxy means tests use household socio-economic indicators to proxy household income or welfare level. In general, the aim is to find one or a few indicators which are less costly to verify, but are sufficiently correlated with income or expenditures to be useful for identifying the poor (Besley and Kanbur, 1993). The advantage of using a few indicators is that administrative costs are kept low, while leakage is less than what it would be under a universal scheme, so that more poverty reduction could be achieved with the same budget (Besley and Kanbur, 1993).

4. Data and methodology

4.1 Data

For our research, we use the Second Malawi Integrated Household Survey (IHS2) data. The NSO (2005b) conducted the IHS2 with the assistance of the International Food Policy Research Institute (IFPRI) and the World Bank. The IHS2 was carried out from March 2004 through March 2005 and covered a sample of 11,280 households that were selected based on a two-stage stratified sampling process and a Probability Proportional to Size (PPS) design. The sample is representative at national as well as district levels.

Furthermore, the survey captures the seasonality in household consumption as the consumption estimates were collected over a period of 13 months. Additionally, a price index was developed by the NSO to account for temporal and spatial price differences in consumption across the country's regions (NSO, 2005b).

In this research, we define poverty as a level of consumption and expenditures that is insufficient for meeting an individual's basic needs in a household. However, such a monetary measure is not a perfect indicator of welfare. Other aspects, such as food security, vulnerability and access to basic services may not be captured by consumption alone, but they are highly correlated with poverty and vulnerability in Malawi (see GoM and World Bank, 2007). Likewise, income and expenditure poverty is the definition adopted by the government of Malawi and the donor community.

4.2 Estimating the models

4.2.1 Estimation method

Due to substantial differences between rural and urban areas, separate models were estimated for rural and urban households. These models were fitted using quantile regression weighted by household weight. Earlier applications of quantile regression include Braithwaite et al. (2000), Zeller and Alcaraz V. (2005), Zeller et al. (2005), and Muller and Bibi, (2008). Quantile regression was first introduced by Koenker and Bassett (Koenker and Hallock, 2001). Defined in the simplest way, quantile regression is a statistical procedure intended to estimate conditional quantile functions in which quantiles of the conditional distribution of the response variable are expressed as functions of observed covariates. In analogy with classical linear regression methods (e.g. ordinary least squares), based on minimizing sums of squared residuals and meant to estimate models for conditional mean functions, quantile regression methods are based on minimizing asymmetrically weighted absolute residuals and are intended to estimate conditional median functions (Buhai, 2004).

The quantile regression was deemed appropriate for estimating the models because we are interested in a particular segment (i.e. the poor) of the analyzed conditional distribution (here the welfare distribution) as a function of several covariates of interest. Furthermore, quantile regression does not impose any sort of strict parametric assumptions on the analyzed distribution. The general form of the model can be expressed as follows:

$$y_i = \beta_j x_{ij} + e_i$$

where y_i *is the dependent variable, i.e. the logarithm of daily per capita expenditures*[52]*;*

x_{ij} *is a set of poverty predictors;*

β_j *is a vector of parameter estimates;*

e_i *is the random error term.*

52 A logarithmic scale was used because it better approximates a normal distribution.

The minimization problem is formulated as follows (Koenker and Hallock, 2001):

$$\min \sum \rho_\tau \left(y_i - \xi\left(x_{ij}, \beta_j \right) \right)$$

where ρ_τ *is a tilted absolute value function with the* τ^{th} *sample quantile as solution.*

$\xi\left(x_{ij}, \beta_j \right)$ *is a linear function of parameters that can be solved by linear programming methods.*

Initially, the set of predictors included 148 indicators[53]. These indicators were selected based on practicability considerations, such as the ease, objectiveness, verifiability and accuracy with which information on the indicators could be quickly elicited in an interview (see, for example, Zeller et al., 2006). The list of selected indicators was then submitted to stepwise regressions out of which the best ten and most significant (at an error level of 1% or less) were retained[54]. Moreover, we controlled for agricultural development districts in order to capture agro-ecological and socioeconomic differences between regions in the rural model.. Likewise, in the urban model, we controlled for the four major cities: Mzuzu, Zomba, Lilongwe, and Blantyre.

Since we are particularly interested in identifying the poor, we estimated the quantile regression at the point of estimation that corresponds to the poverty rate in the population. In that way, the estimation can be said to focus on the poor. We would like to emphasize that the models developed do not seek to identify the determinants of poverty, but select variables that can best approximate the current poverty status of a household. A causal relationship should not be inferred from the results.

4.2.2 Out-of-sample tests

After estimation, out-of-sample validation tests were conducted to assess the predictive power of the models. The main purpose of the validation is to observe how well the models would perform in an independent sample derived from the same population. These tests are good substitutes for direct and very costly field tests that to our knowledge have rarely been used in published research. Without

---

53 The list of indicators included 112 variables in the urban model.

54 Previous researches (Zeller and Alcaraz V., 2005 and Zeller et al., 2005) show that increasing the number of regressors beyond ten only generates marginal improvement in accuracy, while increasing a model's complexity. Therefore, we limited the number of indicators to the best ten.

such validations, the predictive ability of the models on the field would be unknown.

In order to perform the validation tests, we split the initial samples into two sub-samples following the ratio 67:33. The larger samples, or calibration samples, were employed to estimate the models (i.e. identify the best set of variables, their weights, and the optimal cut-offs[55]), whereas the smaller samples, or validation samples, were used to test out-of-sample the predictive accuracy of the models. In the out-of-sample tests, we therefore applied the set of identified indicators, their derived weights and optimal cut-offs to predict the household poverty status. Further robustness tests were conducted by estimating the prediction intervals of the models' performance measures using 1,000 bootstrapped samples[56].

4.2.3 Measuring model targeting performances

Different performance measures can be used to assess the predictive power of a proxy means test model (Table 2).

Table 2. Selected accuracy ratios

Targeting ratios	Definitions
Poverty Accuracy	Total number of households correctly predicted as poor, expressed as a percentage of the total number of poor
Undercoverage	Error of predicting poor households as being non-poor, expressed as a percentage of the total number of poor
Leakage	Error of predicting non-poor households as poor, expressed as a percentage of the total number of poor
Poverty Incidence Error (PIE)	Difference between predicted and actual poverty incidence, measured in percentage points
Balanced Poverty Accuracy Criterion (BPAC)	Poverty accuracy minus the absolute difference between undercoverage and leakage, measured in percentage points

Source: Adapted from IRIS (2005).

55 See Section 4.2.3 for further details on the derivation of the cut-offs.

56 See Efron (1987) for further details on bootstrapping confidence intervals.

Poverty accuracy measures the number of poor correctly predicted by the model, expressed as a percentage of the total number of poor. Undercoverage and leakage are used in the literature to assess the targeting efficiency of development policies (see, for example, Valdivia, 2005; Ahmed et al., 2004; Weiss, 2004). Poverty Incidence Error (PIE) indicates the precision of the model in correctly predicting the poverty incidence.

Balanced Poverty Accuracy Criterion (BPAC) is defined as the poverty accuracy minus the absolute difference between undercoverage and leakage. The BPAC considers the three accuracy measures mentioned above because of their relevance for targeting poverty. These measures exhibit trade-offs. For example, minimizing leakage leads to higher under coverage and lower poverty accuracy. In this paper, the BPAC is used somewhat arbitrarily as the overall criterion to judge a model's overall performance.

In order to estimate the above-mentioned measures, the cut-offs that maximize the BPAC after the models' calibrations were used to predict the household poverty status in the validation samples. Households whose predicted expenditures were higher than the cut-off were predicted/classified as poor, otherwise they were deemed non-poor. This classification was then crossed with the actual household poverty status adopted by the Malawian government (see NSO, 2005a). The latter is defined as follows: households whose daily per capita expenditures were less than Malawi's national poverty line (MK44.29 a day) were classified as *poor,* otherwise they were deemed *non-poor.*

4.3 Policy simulations

It is often argued that targeting is cost-ineffective and once all targeting costs have been considered, a finely targeted program may not be any more cost-efficient and may not have any more effect on poverty than a universal program. Therefore, an evaluation of the costs and benefits of targeting was undertaken using the newly designed system to administer a program which provides cash transfers to Malawi's poor. More importantly, we assessed whether the new system is more target- and cost-efficient than community-based targeting of agricultural subsidy programs in the country.

The total budget required for targeting a transfer scheme can be formulated as follows (Besley and Kanbur, 1993):

$$T = P + NP + A + H$$

Where
T is the total budget of the program;
P is the value of transfers given to the poor;
NP is the value of transfers wrongly given to the non-poor;
A is the administrative costs;
H is the hidden costs (private, indirect, social, and political costs).

Three measures of targeting efficiency are given by:

$$F = P*100/(P + NP).$$
$$F_1 = (NP + A + H)/P;$$
$$F_2 = P*100/(P + NP + A + H);$$

F is the transfer to the poor as a percentage of total transfer;
F_1 is the cost of transferring one unit of resources to the poor;
F_2 is defined as the transfer to the poor as a percentage of total program costs.

Available estimates of administrative costs based on theoretical as well as empirical evaluations range from 0.1% to 30% of total program costs (see Grosh and Baker, 1995; Smith, 2001; Coady, 2003; Smith and Subbarao, 2003). To our knowledge, there is no comprehensive study on the hidden costs of targeting in the literature.

In order to fit with the existing institutional capacity for handling a targeted program, we assumed a realistic transfer scheme to cover 20% of the population; that is approximately the proportion of direct beneficiaries of the Universal Starter Pack (see Smith, 2001). Likewise, we set the total annual budget available for targeting the rural population at US$30 million. This amount is approximately equivalent to the total costs of the Universal Starter Pack and corresponds to about one-third of the costs of the AISP in 2006/2007.

We simulated three transfer schemes (Figure 3) and evaluated their costs, benefits, and poverty impacts based on the models' targeting performances.

Figure 3: Pre- and post-transfer consumption expenditures under different transfer schemes (rural model).

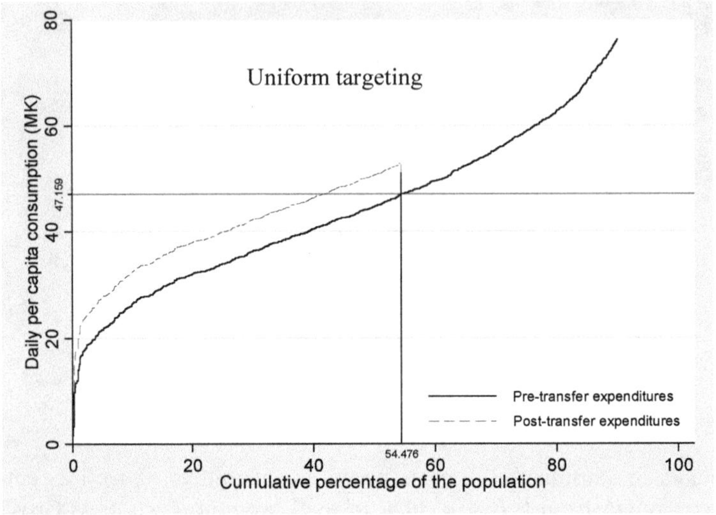

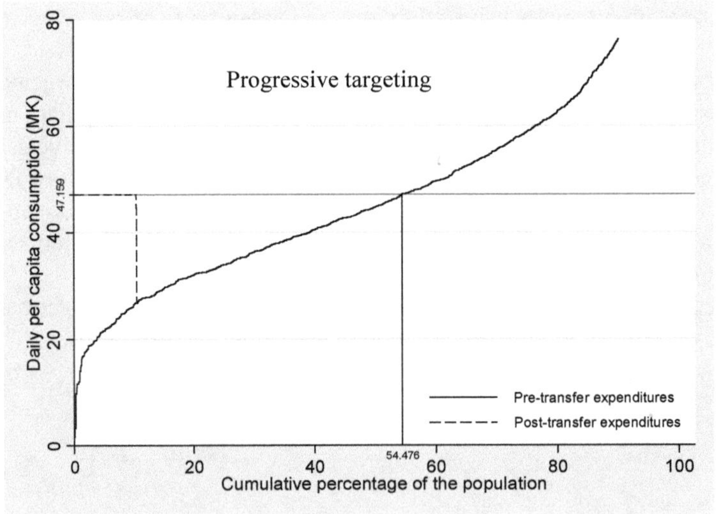

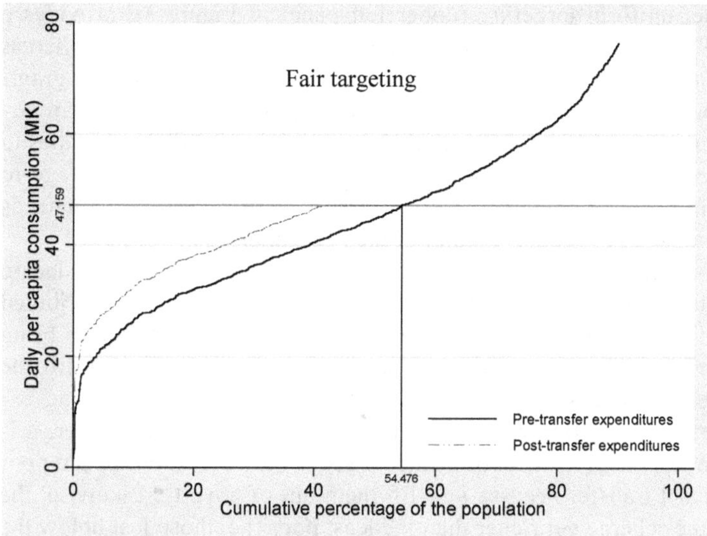

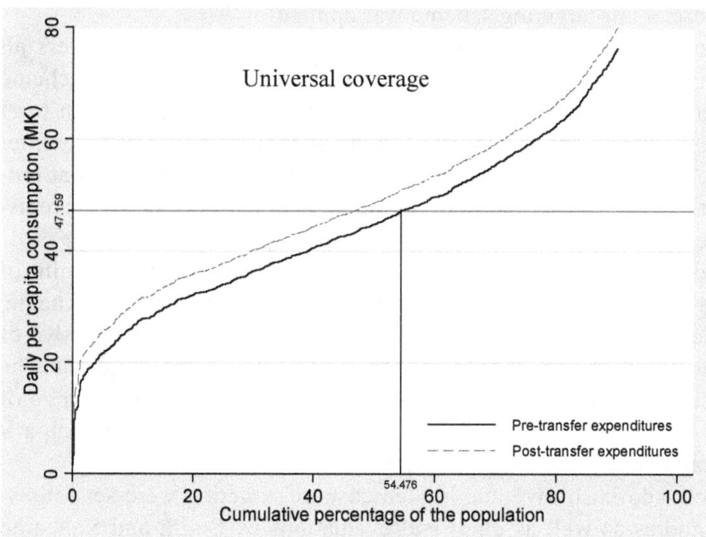

Source: Own results based on Malawi IHS2 data. For a better viewing, the upper 10% of the distribution is not shown in the graph.

The first scheme, uniform targeting (upper left panel of Figure 3), provides a fixed amount of transfer to all poor, irrespective of their poverty level, whereas the second scheme, progressive targeting (upper right panel of Figure 3), grants transfer to the poor progressively according to their poverty level. Uniform targeting is the equivalent of the scheme applied for providing fertilizer subsidies to program beneficiaries in Malawi. Such a scheme reduces excessive leakage to the non-poor, but provides transfers to some less poor in excess of their needs and therefore changes the welfare ranking of the population.

Progressive targeting provides the poorest with the exact transfer needed to bring them up to the poverty line. With this scheme, transfers are distributed from bottom up: first, the poorest poor receives the amount just enough to bring him up to the poverty line, then the next poorest is served, and so on till the available budget (net of costs) is exhausted. This scheme aims at reducing extreme poverty and is more finely targeted than uniform targeting. However, it is more costly than uniform redistribution since it seeks the poorest out of the poor and grants the exact transfer necessary to lift them out of poverty. Likewise, the poorest poor in the scheme get richer than the least poor (i.e. those just below the poverty line) after transfer. As a result, the welfare ranking of the population changes. Therefore, a fair targeting scheme was applied.

The fair targeting scheme (lower left panel of Figure 3) not only covers all poor, but also respects the initial welfare ranking of the population. This scheme provides transfer amounts which ensure that: i) a poorer individual doesn't get richer than its less poor neighbor and ii) all of the poor lifted out of poverty after redistribution lie just at the poverty line, but not above. This scheme aims at preserving the social hierarchy and harmony in the population. It is the finest redistribution scheme.

We compared the benefits and costs of targeting with the reference point of universal coverage (lower right panel of Figure 3). Under the universal scheme, the available budget is distributed equally among the population, irrespective of their poverty status. The universal scheme assumes that there is no targeting. The redistribution schemes applied in this paper are not exhaustive and the range of transfer options is broader, but they do provide some insights into the comparison of welfare gains from different policy choices.

In our research, administrative and hidden costs of targeting were set following theoretical studies as well as empirical evaluations by Smith and Subbarao (2003), Smith (2001), and Besley and Kanbur (1993) who hypothesize that the finer the targeting, the higher the costs of administration[57]. Under a uniform scheme, administrative costs of targeting were estimated at 30% of the budget

57 Confer Section 2.

available for poverty reduction. In addition, we set the hidden costs of targeting at 5% of program administrative costs. Since progressive targeting is finer than uniform targeting, we further increased administrative costs to 35% of the program budget and hidden costs to 10% of administrative costs under the second scheme. Under a fair targeting scheme, administrative and hidden costs are assumed to be identical to the costs under the second scheme, because both schemes provide transfers to the poor in a similar fashion.

Under a universal coverage, we set administrative costs at 50% of the costs of a uniform targeting scheme. In other words, under a universal coverage, administrative costs were set at 15% of total program costs. Likewise, we assumed that under a universal redistribution, the hidden costs of targeting are negligible because everyone is qualified for transfer in that case; no eligibility screening is required. Similarly, under TIP and AISP programs (which were implemented through community-based targeting systems), administrative costs were set at 15% of total program costs. This rate is roughly equivalent to empirical estimates by Dorward et al. (2008). The hidden costs of targeting were estimated at 5% of administrative costs.

We assessed the impacts of targeting on poverty using the Foster-Greer-Thorbecke (FGT)[58] poverty index, which considers the poverty incidence (P_0), the poverty gap (P_1) and the severity of poverty (P_2). Following Ravallion and Chao (1989), we estimated the benefits of targeting as the amount by which an untargeted budget would have to be increased in order to achieve the same targeted poverty level. This amount is the budget difference between a universal and a targeted program which both achieve the same poverty impacts. This estimation assumes that poverty is only tackled directly through the transfers provided. Such an assessment is however, static and underestimates the benefits of targeting which may percolate and strengthen over time through the positive external effects of development on the poor (van de Walle, 1998). A universal program/subsidy (that covers the non-poor) can generate indirect benefits, such as pro-poor market effects (high labor demand and higher casual wages, lower food prices, etc.) that are not realized through a program targeted at the poor only. These considerations require scale and hence the inclusion of non-poor as well. However, measuring all these effects requires additional data and methodological approaches (e.g. general-equilibrium models) that are beyond the scope of this research. Therefore, we limited the evaluation to the direct benefits of targeting. In the case of Malawi, one must emphasize that the indirect effects of a universal program are weakened. Dorward et al. (2008) suggest that Malawi's wealthier farmers did not purchase more fertilizer in the presence of subsidies, but rather

58 See Foster et al. (1984) for a detailed description of the FGT index.

substituted commercial fertilizer for those subsidies, causing substantial market distortions.

5. Empirical results

5.1 How well do the models identify the poor?

Table 3 presents the model results, including the prediction intervals. The parameter estimates are presented in Appendices A and B. These estimates are highly significant. Their signs are consistent with expectations and economic theory.

Table 3. Model targeting performances

Targeting ratios Models	Log cut-off value	Poverty accuracy (%)	Under-coverage (%)	Leakage (%)	PIE (% points)	BPAC (% points)
Rural	3.90	**71.48** (69.3; 73.6)	**28.52** (26.4; 30.7)	**26.65** (23.7; 29.6)	**-0.88** (-0.03; 0.81)	**69.61** (64.5; 72.9)
Urban	3.63	**60.36** (51.5; 69.2)	**39.64** (30.8; 48.5)	**48.65** (34.3; 67.3)	**2.08** (-1.88; 6.15)	**51.35** (32.7; 62.9)

Note: *Poverty accuracy is defined as the number of households correctly predicted as poor by the model, expressed as a percentage of the total number of poor. Undercoverage is defined as the number of poor households predicted as being non-poor, expressed as a percentage of the total number of poor. Leakage is defined as the number of non-poor households predicted as being poor, expressed as a percentage of the total number of poor. PIE or Poverty Incidence Error is the difference between predicted and actual poverty incidence, measured in percentage points. BPAC is defined as the poverty accuracy minus the absolute difference between undercoverage and leakage, measured in percentage points.*

Source: *Own results based on Malawi IHS2 data. Prediction intervals in brackets.*

Table 3 shows that the rural model yields a poverty accuracy of 71.48% and a BPAC of 69.61 percentage points. This result indicates that the model would cover about 71% of the poor if used for Malawi's poor. The model's undercoverage is estimated at about 28.52%, while its leakage is set at 26.65% which means that the model would leak benefits to about 27% of the non-poor. The PIE nears 0 percentage points, which implies that the model perfectly predicts the observed poverty rate out-of-sample. With regard to the urban model, the same trend applies. However, its estimated BPAC is lower (51.35 percentage points) as compared with the rural model and only 60% of the urban poor are covered. Also, leakage is high (48.65%) under the model. Section 5.2 analyzes the cost-effectiveness and impacts of targeting.

5.2. Targeting performances of development policies

Table 4 compares the targeting performances of the rural model with the performances of TIP and 2006/2007 AISP, both of which were administered through community-based targeting mechanisms in rural Malawi.

Table 4. Comparison of the targeting efficiency of TIP and AISP versus the new system

Program type	Poverty accuracy (%)	Undercoverage (%)	Leakage (%)
Universal program	100	0	112.18
2000/2001 TIP[a]	65.02	34.98	61.81
2006/2007 AISP	54	46	54
New system (rural model)	71.48	28.52	26.65

Note: *TIP denotes Targeted Input Program. AISP denotes Agricultural Input Support Program. Poverty accuracy is defined as the number of poor who received program benefits (under TIP and AISP) or the number of poor who were predicted as being poor (under the new system), expressed as a percentage of the total number of poor. Undercoverage is defined as the number of poor households who did not receive program benefits (under TIP and AISP) or the number of poor who were predicted as being non-poor (under the new system), expressed as a percentage of the total number of poor. Leakage is defined as the number of non-poor households who received program benefits (under TIP and AISP) or the number of non-poor who were predicted as being poor (under the new system), expressed as a percentage of the total number of poor.*

a *Main cropping season and rural areas estimates.*

Source: *Own results based on Malawi IHS2 data plus estimates based on Dorward et al. (2008).*

Table 4 indicates that under the new system, about 71% of poor households would be correctly targeted and receive agricultural inputs compared with 65% and 54% of the poor who actually received TIP and AISP benefits, respectively. The undercoverage rate of the new system is also low (29%) compared with both targeted programs. More importantly, the results suggest that TIP and AISP exhibit substantial leakages of fertilizer and seeds to non-poor households as their leakage rates amount to 62% and 54%, respectively, against 27% under the new proxy model. This result implies that under the new system, leakage could potentially be cut by two-thirds. However, the comparison of the new system with TIP and AISP did not consider implementation aspects and the political reality that decision makers or program managers may adjust targeting criteria or the list of beneficiaries due to political, administrative, budgetary, or other reasons. These issues are critical here, as we compared actual targeting measures with modeled outcomes assuming flawless implementation. Our focus is not on the implementation of TIP and AISP (see Dorward et al., 2008; Harrigan, 2008; Levy and Barahona, 2002 for details on the implementation of TIP and AISP), but rather on alternative targeting mechanisms that might be considered by policy makers for implementation (first in pilot programs, later countrywide).

Any targeting strategy is prone to facing implementation difficulties due to political processes and information asymmetries. Furthermore, the actual outcomes of a newly proposed targeting methodology can only be assessed through experimental action research, ideally with the exact replication of the proposed targeting process with all institutions involved in distributing subsidies. Such action research is beyond the scope of this paper as it would require cooperation between government agencies and pilot communities, complemented by household and other surveys.

Nonetheless, we assert that implementation difficulties are lower with our proposed models because the indicators used are more precise and easier to measure (see Appendices A and B) by targeting agents compared with TIP and AISP selection criteria which are quite loosely defined and leave much judgement to the community.[59]

5.3 Evaluating the cost-effectiveness and impacts of targeting the poor: Policy simulations[60]

5.3.2 Cost-efficiency, benefits, and impacts of targeting

In this section, we analyze the cost-effectiveness and impacts of targeting using the models developed. The magnitude of targeting costs, benefits, and impact depends on the program budget, the model accuracy, the total number of poor,

59 See Dorward et al. (2008) and Chinsinga (2005a, b) for further details on the targeting criteria used by TIP and AISP.

60 For brevity reasons, only the simulation results for the rural model are presented.

and the depth of poverty in the population. Table 5 presents the transfer efficiency and poverty impacts of targeting[61].

Table 5. Transfer efficiency and poverty impacts of targeting

Indicators / Models		Transfer efficiency			Post-transfer poverty (poverty impacts)		
		F	F_1	F_2	P_o	P_1	P_2
Rural model							
Universal coverage		54.48	1.16	46.30	46.96 (-7.52)	0.11 (-0.04)	5.73 (-3.08)
Targeted program	scheme 1	80.0	0.83	54.80	41.58 (-12.90)	0.08 (-0.07)	4.45 (-4.36)
	scheme 2	87.54	0.86	53.83	44.05 (-10.42)	0.09 (-0.06)	3.79 (-5.02)
	scheme 3	77.66	1.09	47.76	41.49 (-12.99)	0.09 (-0.06)	4.34 (-4.48)

Note: F is the transfer to the poor as a percentage of total transfer. F_1 is the cost of transferring one unit of resources to the poor. F_2 is defined as the transfer to the poor as a percentage of the total program costs. P_0 is the poverty incidence; P_1 is the poverty gap; and P_2 is the severity of poverty. Baseline poverty measures are estimated at P_o= 54.48%; P_1 = 0.15; P_2= 8.81. Poverty impacts (in brackets) are measured as post minus pre-transfer poverty.

Source: Own results based on Malawi IHS2 data.

Table 5 suggests that transfer efficiency and post-transfer poverty improve under targeted schemes compared with universal coverage. The transfer to the poor as a percentage of total transfer (F) and the transfer to the poor as a percentage of total program costs (F_2) increase, whereas the costs per unit of resources transferred (F1) decrease under a targeted scheme compared with universal coverage. For instance, under universal coverage the program spends MK1.16 for every MK transferred to the poor, as opposed to MK0.83, MK0.86, and MK1.09 under uniform, progressive, and fair targeting, respectively. Likewise, the transfer to the poor as a percentage of total program costs increases from 46.30% under universal coverage to 54.8%, 53.83%, and 47.76% under uniform, progressive, and fair targeting, respectively. Table 5 also indicates that the transfer efficiency differs considerably between targeted and untargeted regimes with exceptions. Under a fair targeting scheme, F_1 and F_2 do not improve much compared with universal coverage because of higher costs.

61 Cost estimates are provided in Appendix C.

Similarly, the finest redistribution doesn't consistently yield the best transfer efficiency, nor does it consistently improve post-transfer poverty. In other words, even though progressive targeting provides the highest transfer (F) to the poor, it yields the lowest poverty impacts on P_o (i.e. the highest post-transfer poverty). Conversely, fair targeting which yields the lowest efficiency (F) achieves the highest poverty impacts in terms of P_o. For instance, under fair targeting, the poverty incidence (P_o) is reduced by 13%, as compared with 10% under progressive targeting. Conversely, under progressive targeting, the severity of poverty (P_2) is reduced by 5.02, versus 4.48 under fair targeting. These results are driven by the difference between both redistribution schemes: under progressive targeting, a higher total transfer lifts fewer poorer people out of poverty, whereas a lower total transfer lifts many less poor out of poverty under fair targeting. As concerns the poverty gap (P_1), there are no sizable differences between the targeting schemes applied.

What are the benefits of targeting? Table 6 attempts to answer the question.

Table 6. Benefits from targeting

Costs and benefits / Post-transfer poverty		Total costs: Targeted program	Total costs: Universal coverage	Direct benefits
	Po = **41.58** (scheme 1)	3552.6	5550.73	1998.13 (6.8%)
Poverty level	Po ≈ **44.054** (scheme 2)	3552.6	4389.09	836.49 (2.3%)
	Po = **41.49** (scheme 3)	3552.6	5601.60	2049.29 (6.9%)

Note: P_0 is the poverty incidence; P_1 is the poverty gap; and P_2 is the severity of poverty. Direct benefits are measured as the amount by which an untargeted program would have to be increased in order to achieve the same targeted poverty level P_0. The budget available for poverty reduction is set at US$30 million. The figures in brackets indicate the additional reduction of poverty achievable with the direct benefits. Cost estimates are given in million Malawi Kwacha (MK) using 2005 prices. US$1 = MK118.42.

Source: Own results based on Malawi IHS2 data.

Table 6 suggests that targeting Malawi's poor with the new system is potentially beneficial: with a targeted program, fewer resources can achieve the post-transfer poverty attained under universal coverage. Furthermore, Table 6 indicates that the higher the impact on poverty – the lower the post-transfer poverty (Po) -, the higher the benefits from targeting. In other words, the scheme that reduces the poverty incidence the most yields the highest targeting benefits. Likewise, the results show that progressive targeting does not necessarily increase the benefits from targeting (compared with uniform targeting). For example, a universal coverage would cost MK4.40 billion, whereas a progressive scheme would cost only MK3.553 billion if it were to achieve a post-transfer poverty of 44% (Scheme 2). Thus, the benefits from targeting are estimated at MK836.49 million.

On other hand, achieving a post-transfer poverty rate (Po) of 41.58% under uniform targeting would result in total benefit of MK1.998 billion compared with universal coverage. Further simulations show that the benefits derived from uniform targeting (Scheme 1) would further reduce the poverty incidence by 6.8%, whereas the benefits from progressive and fair targeting (Schemes 2 and 3) would reduce the poverty incidence by 2.3% and 6.9%, respectively, if these benefits were uniformly targeted at the poor.

5.4 Cost efficiency of targeted agricultural input support programs versus the new system

Would the new proxy system be more cost-efficient if it were used to target Malawi's past agricultural input subsidy programs? Table 7 compares the cost-effectiveness of those (p.116).

Table 7 shows that under community-based targeting, TIP transferred an average amount of MK772 (input equivalent) to the poor versus MK811 with the new system. The costs of leakage are cut down by 55% compared with TIP; from MK535 million to MK242 million. Estimates of the transfer efficiency measures also suggest that administering TIP with the new system would have been more efficient, transferring 72% of total transfer to the poor (i.e. 50% of program costs) compared with 51% (i.e. 43% of program costs) under community-based targeting. Likewise, with the new system, MK1 is spent for every MK transferred to the poor, as opposed to MK1.32 under community-based targeting. The same trend applies to the AISP with one exception: under the new system, average transfer per poor decreases (though the total transfer to the poor increases): more poor have been covered by the program, but the increase in total transfer to the poor (under the new system) is less proportional to the increase in program coverage.

Table 7. Costs and transfer efficiency of TIP and AISP versus the new system

Costs / Programs	Total transfer to the poor[c]	Costs of leakage	Adminis-trative costs	Hidden costs	Total costs	F	F_1	F_2
2000/2001 TIP[a]	562.61 (772.11)	534.84	195.39	9.77	1302.62	51.27	1.32	43.19
TIP with new system	649.97 (811.33)	242.33	390.79	19.54	1302.62	72.84	1.00	49.90
2006/2007 AISP[b]	2777.51 (4397.33)	2940.89	1018.11	50.91	6787.41	48.57	1.44	40.92
AISP with new system	3386.71 (3825.58)	1262.67	2036.22	101.81	6787.41	72.84	1.00	49.90

Note: *TIP denotes Targeted Input Program. AISP denotes Agricultural Input Support Program. F is the transfer to the poor as a percentage of total transfer. F_1 is the cost of transferring one unit of program resources to the poor. F_2 is defined as the transfer to the poor as a percentage of the total program costs. The cost estimates are given in million Malawi Kwacha (MK), the national currency in Malawi. [a]TIP cost estimates are based on Smith (2001). [b]Estimates of the net cost of main fertilizer (Urea and NPK) subsidy are based on Dorward et al. (2008). [c]The average transfer per household (in brackets) is given in MK. The costs of leakage are defined as the amount of transfer wrongly given to the non-poor. Administrative costs are the costs of running the program. The hidden costs include: private, indirect, social, and political costs (see Besley and Kanbur, 1993 for further details on these costs).*

Source: *Own results based on Malawi IHS2 data.*

Overall, the above results show that the proposed targeting system can potentially improve the cost and transfer efficiency of the country's development programs compared with the currently used mechanisms for delivering benefits to the poor and smallholder farmers. However, there is scope for further improvement; the system is not perfect at targeting. The system can be shared between several programs and/or combined with other methods in a multi-stage targeting process. For example, the system can be combined with geographical targeting to improve accuracy and to target regions with disproportionate numbers of poor. The estimation of separate models for urban and rural areas in this paper illustrates such a combination. Misreporting can be reduced with an effective verification system, including random home visits, triangulation of the information provided by potential program beneficiaries, introduction of bonus and malus clauses for targeting agents, etc. The observed leakage can be recouped through the taxation of the non-poor (see, for example, Besley and Kanbur, 1993).

6. Conclusions and policy implications

This paper assesses the cost-effectiveness and impacts of indicator-based targeting in Malawi. The conclusion that emerges from the results is that targeting the poor and smallholder farmers through proxy means tests is potentially more target-, cost- and impact-efficient than universal interventions and the currently used mechanisms for targeting the country's agricultural subsidies. Though administrative costs increase under the proposed proxy means system, the results indicate that the overall benefits may well outweigh the costs of targeting. Likewise, under an indicator-based system, targeted programs appear to concentrate more resources on the country's poor and have the highest impact on poverty.

More importantly, estimation results suggest that the newly designed proxy system is potentially more target- and cost-efficient when used for targeting the 2000/01 Targeted Input Program (TIP) and the 2006/07 Agricultural Input Support Program (AISP). Thus, the new system may improve the targeting and cost-efficiency of development programs and hence reduce the displacement of commercial fertilizers in the country. However, such improvements are possible only if targeted programs are fairly well implemented. The issue of implementation is critical here, as our results and conclusions assume a perfect implementation of the proposed targeting system, whereas TIP and AISP performances are based on actual program outcomes. Even though the effect of actual implementation cannot be strongly asserted, it may weaken the performances of the proposed system. Nonetheless, the findings in this paper suggest that indicator-based targeting may be worth the effort and may improve program targeting and cost efficiency.

This work is prospectively relevant for Malawi as its policy makers reflect on improving the efficiency of the country's pro-poor development programs. The research could also be applied in other developing countries with similar targeting problems, as well as in those that are considering introducing targeted subsidy schemes for the poor and smallholder farmers.

References

Ahmed, A., Rashid, S., Sharma, M. Zohir, S., 2004. Food aid distribution in Bangladesh: Leakage and operational performance. Discussion paper No. 173. Washington. D.C.: The International Food Policy Research Institute.

Besley, T., Kanbur, R., 1993. The principles of targeting, in: Lipton, M., Van Der Gaag, J. (Eds.), Including the Poor. pp. 67-90. Proceedings of a symposium organized by the World Bank and the International Food Policy Research Institute, Washington D.C.

Braithwaite, J. Grootaert, C., Milanovic, B., 2000. Poverty and Social Assistance in Transition Countries. Saint Martin's Press, New York.

Buhai, S., 2004. Quantile regression: Overview and selected applications. Tinbergen Institute and Erasmus University, Rotterdam.

Chinsinga, B., 2005a. The clash of voices: Community-based targeting of safety-net interventions in Malawi. Social Policy and Administration 39 (3), 284-301.

Chinsinga, B., 2005b. Practical and policy dilemmas in targeting free inputs: in Levy, S. (Ed.), Starter Packs: A strategy to Fight Hunger in Developing and Transition Countries? Lessons from the Malawi Experience, 1998-2003, CAB International, Wallingford.

Coady, D., Parker, S., 2009. Targeting performance under self-selection and administrative targeting methods. Economic Development and Cultural Change 57 (3), 559-587.

Coady, D., 2003. Cost-effective safety nets: What are the costs of reaching the poor? World Issue brief. World Food Program and International Food Policy Research Institute: Washington D.C.

Coady, D., Grosh, M., Hoddinott, J., 2004. Targeting outcomes redux. The World Bank Research Observer 19 (1), 61-85.

Coady, D., Grosh, M., Hodinott, J., 2002. The Targeting of Transfer in Developing Countries: Review of Experiences and Lessons. Washington D.C.: The World Bank.

Conning, J., Kevanne, M., 2002. Community-based targeting mechanisms for social safety nets: A critical review. World Development 30 (3), 375-394.

Dorward, A., Chirwa, E., Kelly, V., Jayne, T., Slater, R., Duncan, B., 2008. Evaluation of the 2006/07 Agricultural Input Subsidy Programme. Final report, Malawi.

Dutrey, A. P., 2007. Successful targeting? Reporting efficiency and costs in targeted poverty alleviation programs. Program paper No. 35. United Nations Research Institute for Social Development (UNRISD), Geneva.

Efron, B.,1987. Better bootstrap confidence intervals. Journal of the American Statistical Association 82 (397), 171-185.

Foster, J., Greer, J., Thorbecke, E., 1984. A class of decomposable poverty measures. Econometrica 52 (3), 761-766.

Government of Malawi., World Bank., 2007. Malawi Poverty and Vulnerability Assessment Report: Investing in our Future. Synthesis report, Malawi.

Grosh, M. E., Baker, J. L., 1995. Proxy means tests for targeting social programs: Simulations and speculation. Working paper No. 118. Washington D.C.: The World Bank.

Harrigan, J., 2008. Food insecurity, poverty and the Malawian Starter Pack: Fresh start or false start? Food Policy 33 (3), 237-249.

Hoddinott, J., 1999. Targeting: Principles and practices. Technical guide, Washington D.C.: The International Food Policy Research Institute.

IRIS., 2005. Note on Assessment and Improvement of Tool Accuracy. Mimeograph, revised version from June 2, 2005. IRIS Center, University of Maryland, USA.

Koenker, R. and Hallock, K. F., 2001. Quantile regression. Journal of Economic Perspectives 15 (4), 143-156.

Lawson, M., Cullen, A., Sibale, B., Ligomeka, S., Lwanda, F., 2001. Targeted Inputs Programme (TIP): Findings of the Monitoring Component for TIP 2000-2001. Report commissioned to the Ministry of Agriculture and Irrigation (Malawi) by the Department for International Development, UK.

Levy, S., Barahona, C., 2002. Targeted Inputs Programme (TIP): Main Report of the Evaluation Programme. Report submitted to the Ministry of Agriculture and Irrigation (Malawi) and the Department for International Development, UK.

Minde, I., Jayne, T. S., Crawford, E., Ariga, J., Govereh, J., 2008. Promoting fertilizer use in Africa: Current issues and empirical evidence from Malawi, Zambia, and Kenya. Working paper No. 13. Regional Strategic Analysis and Knowledge Support System (ReSAKSS), Pretoria, South Africa.

Muller, C., Bibi, S., 2008. Focused targeting against poverty: Evidence from Tunisia. University of Cergy-Pontoise, Faculté des Sciences Economiques et de Gestion de Tunis.

National Statistics Office., 2005a. Malawi Integrated Household Survey 2004-2005. Zomba, Malawi.

National Statistics Office., 2005b. Malawi Second Integrated Household Survey (IHS2): Basic information document. Zomba, Malawi.

Ravallion, M., Chao, K., 1989. Targeted policies for poverty alleviation under imperfect information: Algorithms and applications. Journal of Policy Modelling 11 (2), 213-224.

Ricker-Gilbert, J., Jayne, T. S., 2009. Do fertilizer subsidies affect the demand for commercial fertilizer? An example from Malawi. Paper presented at the 27th International Association of Agricultural Economists (IAAE) Conference, 12- 18 August 2009 Beijing, China.

Rook, J., Freeland, N., 2006. Targeting social transfers. Regional Hunger and Vulnerability Program (WAHENGA).

Smith, J. W., 2001. Spending on safety nets for the poor: How much, for how many? The case of Malawi. Africa Region Working paper No. 11. Washington D.C.: The World Bank.

Smith, J.W., Subbarao, K., 2003. What role for safety net transfers in very low income countries. Social Protection Discussion paper No. 030, World Bank Institute Washington D.C.: The World Bank.
Valdivia, M., 2005. Is identifying the poor the main problem in targeting nutritional program? Discussion paper No. 7. Washington D.C.: The World Bank.
van de Walle, D., 1998. Targeting revisited. The World Bank Research Observer 13 (2), 231-248.
Weiss, J., 2004. Reaching the poor with poverty projects: What is the evidence on social returns? Research paper No. 61. Tokyo: The Asian Development Bank Institute.
World Bank., 2009a. World Development Indicators. Washington D.C.: The World Bank.
World Bank., 2009b. Malawi – country brief. www.worldbank.org. (Accessed September 11, 2009).
World Bank., 2007. Malawi social protection status report, No 40027-MW. Sustainable Development Network, Africa region. Washington D.C.: The World Bank.
World Bank., 2006. Malawi: Public works program – conditional cash transfers as an emergency response to a national food shortage. Washington D.C.: The World Bank.
Zeller, M., Sharma, M., Henry, C., Lapenu, C., 2006. An operational tool for assessing the poverty outreach performance of development policies and projects: Results of case studies in Africa, Asia, and Latin America. World Development 34 (3), 446-464.
Zeller, M., Alcaraz, V. G., 2005. Developing and Testing Poverty Assessment Tools: Results from Accuracy Tests in Uganda. IRIS Center, University of Maryland, USA.
Zeller, M., Alcaraz, V. G., Johannsen, J., 2005. Developing and Testing Poverty Assessment Tools: Results from Accuracy Tests in Bangladesh. IRIS Center, University of Maryland, USA.

Annexes

Annex 1. Quantile regression results (rural model)

Wald statistic = 3377.251***		Likelihood ratio: 3082.501***		
Point of estimation: 56.408		Number of observations= 6560		
Dependent variable: Logarithm of daily per capita expenditures				
Indicator set		Parameter estimates	Standard errors	T-values
	Intercept	4.337***	0.045	96.88
Control variables	Agricultural development district Mzuzu	-0.015	0.048	-0.32
	Agricultural development district Kasungu	0.184***	0.042	4.38
	Agricultural development district Salima	-0.028	0.048	-0.59
	Agricultural development district Lilongwe	0.090**	0.044	2.07
	Agricultural development district Machinga	-0.237***	0.043	-5.53
	Agricultural development district Blantyre	-0.156***	0.043	-3.66
	Agricultural development district Ngabu	-0.154***	0.055	-2.80
Best 10 indicators	1. Household size	-0.154***	0.004	-43.25
	2. Wireless radio ownership	0.109***	0.014	7.60
	3. Floor of main dwelling is predominantly made of smoothed cement	0.360***	0.022	16.16
	4. Bicycle ownership	0.148***	0.016	9.32
	5. Lighting fuel is electricity	0.631***	0.065	9.69
	6. Panga ownership	0.084***	0.015	5.75
	7. Highest educational qualification acquired in household is Junior Certificate of Education (JCE)	0.120***	0.028	4.31
	8. Does any household member sleep under a bed net?	0.121***	0.015	8.32
	9. Rubbish disposal facility is public heap	-0.082***	0.019	-4.32
	10. Household head can read Chichewa language	0.117***	0.015	7.87

Note: *A panga is a large heavy knife used for cutting vegetation. *** denotes significant at the 99% level. ** denotes significant at the 95% level.*

Source: *Own results based on Malawi IHS2 data.*

Annex 2. Quantile regression results (urban model)

Wald statistic = 880.603***	Likelihood ratio: 1017.934***
Point of estimation: 24.685	Number of observations= 960

Dependent variable: Logarithm of daily per capita expenditures

	Indicator set	Parameter estimates	Standard errors	T-values
	Intercept	4.467***	0.112	40.04
Control variables	Lilongwe city	-0.052	0.066	-0.79
	Zomba city	-0.324***	0.080	-4.05
	Blantyre city	-0.187***	0.065	-2.89
Best 10 indicators	1. Household size	-0.220**	0.015	-14.52
	2. Household has no toilet facility	-0.289**	0.113	-2.56
	3. Household has a cellular phone in working condition	0.625***	0.064	9.81
	4. Number of separate rooms occupied by household, excluding toilet, storeroom, or garage	0.124***	0.022	5.74
	5. Household head can read Chichewa language	-0.134**	0.065	2.06
	6. Sewing machine ownership	0.243***	0.093	2.62
	7. Highest class level ever attended by members is superior or post-secondary	0.492***	0.098	5.03
	8. Main source of cooking fuel is collected firewood	-0.317***	0.058	-5.50
	9. Lighting fuel is electricity	0.366***	0.060	6.12
	10. Floor of main dwelling is predominantly made of smoothed cement	0.181***	0.050	3.65

Note: *** denotes significant at the 99% level. ** denotes significant at the 95% level.
Source: Own results based on Malawi IHS2 data.

Annex 3. Costs of targeting

Costs / Schemes	Total transfer to the poor*	Costs of leakage to the non-poor	Administrative costs	Hidden costs	Total costs
Universal coverage (Zero targeting)	1645.02 (1395.58)	1374.69	532.89	0	3552.6
Uniform targeting (Scheme 1)	1946.80 (2180.50)	486.74	1065.78	53.29	3552.6
Progressive targeting (Scheme 2)	1912.52 (2142.12)	272.32	1243.41	124.34	3552.6
Fair targeting (Scheme 3)	1696.74 (1900.43)	488.11	1243.41	124.34	3552.6

Note: *The cost estimates are given in million Malawi Kwacha (MK) using 2005 prices, US$1= MK118.42.*
*The budget available for poverty reduction is set at US$30 million. *The average transfer per poor (in brackets) is given in MK.*

Source: *Own results based on Malawi IHS2 data.*

Chapter V: General Conclusions

This book explores potential models that might improve the targeting and cost efficiency of development programs in Malawi. Most previous programs in the country have been targeted through community-based targeting systems in which local authorities and community leaders select program beneficiaries based on their assessment of household living conditions. However, they have been characterized by poor targeting: they cover limited numbers of poor and leak program benefits to significant numbers of non-poor. To reverse this trend, the research in this volume proposes targeting by proxy means tests. Proxy means tests seek a few indicators that can be easily verified and sufficiently correlate with income to be useful for targeting the poor (Besley and Kanbur, 1993). Compared with the currently used targeting mechanisms in the country, proxy means tests have the merit of making replicable judgments using consistent and visible criteria (Coady et *al.*, 2002).

The research draws on the Malawi Second Integrated Household (IHS2) survey data of 2004/2005. The IHS2 is a nationally representative survey which covered 11,280 households and a wide range of household socioeconomic indicators (NSO, 2005b). The criteria for the selection of indicators for the models were based on Zeller et *al.* (2006) and included practicability criteria regarding the ease and accuracy with which information on the indicators can be quickly elicited in an interview as well as considerations regarding the objectiveness and verifiability of an indicator. Using Weighted Least Square, Weighted Logit, and Quantile regression methods along with stepwise selection of variables, the book develops empirical models for improving the poverty outreach of agricultural and development programs in Malawi. Furthermore, the research assesses the robustness or predictive power of the models using out-of-sample tests. To conduct these tests, the initial samples were split into two sub-samples – a calibration and a validation samples – following the ratio 67/33 and the same stratification as the original sample. In addition, the prediction intervals were estimated using bootstrapped simulation methods. Bootstrap is the statistical procedure which models sampling from a population by the process of resampling from the sample (Hall, 1994). Unlike standard confidence interval estimation, bootstrap does not make any distributional assumption about the population and hence does not require the assumption of normality. The models developed were calibrated to three poverty lines: the national, international, and extreme poverty lines.

It is often argued that targeting is cost-ineffective and once all targeting costs have been considered, a finely targeted program may not be any more cost-efficient and may not have any more impact on poverty than a universal program. Therefore, we estimated the cost-effectiveness and impacts of targeting the poor. Furthermore, we assessed whether the newly developed system of targeting is more efficient both in terms of targeting performances and costs than the Targeted Input Program (TIP) and the 2006/2007 Agricultural Input Subsidy Program (AISP).

Estimation results suggest that under the new system, mis-targeting is considerably reduced and targeting performances improve compared with the currently used mechanisms in the country. All of the three estimation methods applied achieve approximately the same level of targeting performances out-of-sample. The rural model achieves an average poverty accuracy of about 72% and a leakage rate of 27% when calibrated to the national poverty line of MK44.29. On the other hand, the urban model yields on average a poverty accuracy of about 62% and a leakage rate of 39% under the same poverty line. These results are consistent with the Receiver Operating Characteristic (ROC) curves of the models which show that there is no sizable difference in aggregate predictive accuracy between the estimation methods. ROC curves are powerful tools for estimating the number of poor a program should reach and the number of non-poor that would also be wrongly targeted. Calibrating the models to a higher poverty line improves targeting performances, while calibrating the models to a lower line does the opposite. For example, under the international poverty line of US$1.25 (i.e. MK59.18 PPP), the rural model covers about 82% of the poor and wrongly targets only 16% of non-poor, whereas the urban model covers about 74% of the poor and wrongly identifies 26% of non-poor. On the other hand, using an extreme poverty line of MK29.81 disappointingly reduces the model poverty accuracy and leakage: the rural model yields a poverty accuracy of 51% and a leakage rate of 39% while the urban model yields a poverty accuracy of about 48% and a leakage rate of 68%.

Irrespective of the estimation method and poverty line, the models yield some targeting errors, though the errors decrease with increasing poverty line. A breakdown of targeting errors by poverty deciles indicates that the models perform well in terms of those who are mistargeted; covering most of the poorest deciles and excluding most of the richest ones. The presence of targeting errors does however, point to a fundamental issue: proxy means tests can improve the poverty outreach of a development program, but like any other targeting method, they are not a perfect device for identifying the poor. It is all important to emphasize that a core objective of this research is to predict, but not to infer a causal relationship on poverty. Therefore, the proxy means test models developed can only predict poverty, but cannot explain it.

Simulation results suggest that targeting Malawi's poor and smallholder farmers is more cost- and impact-effective compared with universal coverage. Better targeting not only reduces the Malawian Government's direct costs for providing benefits, but also reduces the total cost of a targeted program. Finer targeting concentrates resources on the poor, whereas under universal coverage, benefits spread thin. Though administrative costs increase with finer targeting, the results indicate that the overall benefits outweigh the costs of targeting. Likewise, finer targeting reduces the costs of leakage by a sizable margin and produces the highest impacts on poverty. However, the finest redistribution does not consistently yield the best transfer efficiency, nor does it consistently improve post-transfer poverty.

More importantly, the newly designed system appears to be more target- and cost-efficient than TIP and AISP. While TIP and AISP transferred about 50% of total transfer, under the new system about 73% of transfer are delivered to the poor and smallholder farmers. Likewise, under the new proxy system, the costs of leakage are cut by 55% and 57% for TIP and AISP, respectively. Thus, with the new system it is possible to reduce leakage and undercoverage rates and improve the cost and transfer efficiency of development programs in the country.

In general, the sets of proxy indicators selected are consistent with the local communities' understandings of poverty. They are objective and most can be easily verified. They broadly include the poverty indicators perceived by Malawian households as important correlates of their welfare (see for example Benson et *al.*, 2006). However, the collection of information on these indicators might entail an effective verification process to reduce bribery, misreports, and fraudulent information from the enumerators as well as potential beneficiaries who may intentionally provide false information to qualify for program benefits.

There are various ways on how to reduce the observed targeting errors and costs and further improve the efficiency of targeting by the proxy means test system. Administrative costs could be cut by sharing the same system between several programs or by combining different targeting methods. Likewise, as others have mentioned, the costs of leakage can be reduced by recouping through taxation of the non-poor. Proper implementation mechanisms and management options can help reduce targeting errors and program costs. Indeed, implementation is an important determinant of targeting performance (Coady et *al.*, 2004).

Valid proxy indicators are difficult to establish. The fact that we stress the use of proxy means tests in this research does not imply that other potential targeting methods should be disregarded. Indeed, targeting methods are not mutually exclusive and may work better in combination. Therefore, the system developed can be combined with other methods in a multi-stage targeting process. For example, geographical targeting can be used to select regions with disproportionate number of poor within Malawi and then the proxy means system can be used to screen households within the selected regions. The estimation of separate models for rural and urban areas of Malawi implies to some extent a combination of geographical and proxy means targeting.

The models developed offer a better alternative for targeting the poor and smallholder farmers in Malawi. They can be used in a wide range of applications, such as:

- *improving the existing targeting mechanisms of farm input subsidy program which relies on community-based targeting systems;*
- *assessing household eligibility to welfare programs and safety net benefits;*
- *producing estimates of poverty rates and monitoring changes in poverty over time as the country and donors cannot afford the costs of frequent and comprehensive household consumption expenditure surveys and;*
- *assessing the poverty outreach of microfinance institutions operating in the country.*

This broad range of applications makes the models potential policy tools for the country. Though the models developed have proven their validity, they remain to be tested for robustness across time. Likewise, a number of other potential estimation methods can be explored to develop proxy means test models. These include: Classification and Regression Trees (CART), Support Vector Machines (SVM), neural networks, etc. Reducing poverty requires first identifying the poor. However, the proxy indicator system developed is not sufficient. It must also be coupled with investments in education, rural infrastructure, economic growth related sectors, and strong political will to impact on the welfare of Malawians.

General Appendices

Appendix 1. Map of Malawi

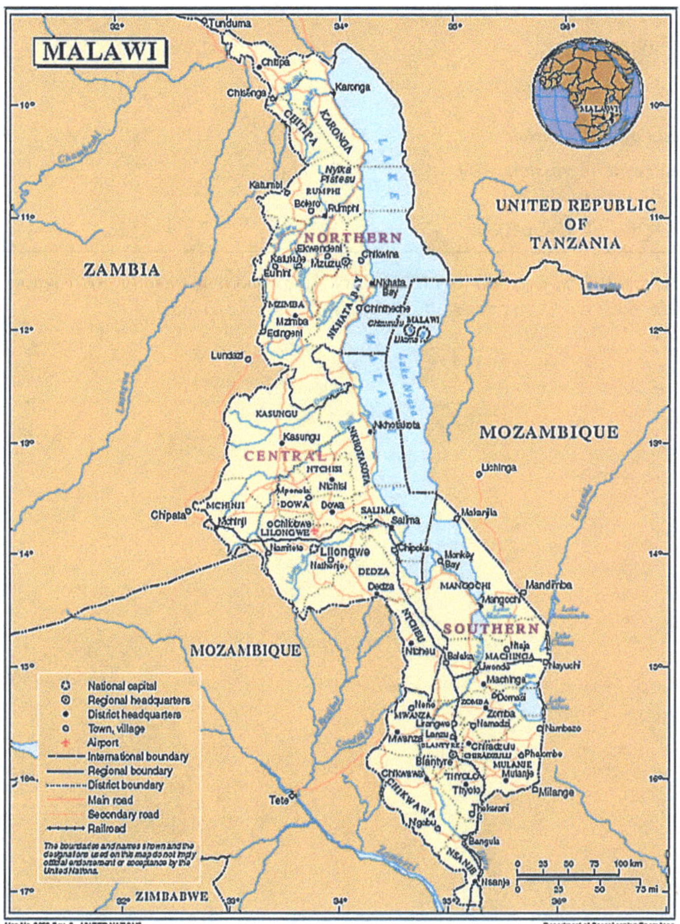

Source: National Statistics Office (2005)

Appendix 2. Sample size and number of potential indicators by model type and estimation method

Sub-samples	Rural model	Urban model	Total
Total sample size	9,840	1,440	11,280
Calibration sample (2/3 observations)	6,560	960	7,540
Validation sample (1/3 observations)	3,280	480	3,760
Number of indicators			
Weighted Least Square Regression	148	112	-
Weighted Logit Regression	148	112	-
Weighted Logit Regression with categorical predictors only	98	79	-
Weighted Quantile Regression	148	112	-

Source: Own results based on Malawi IHS2 data. All estimations include seven regional dummies for the rural model and three city dummies for the urban model.

Appendix 3. Descriptive statistics of variables used in the rural model (full sample)

Variable label	Minimum	Maximum	Mean	Median	Standard Deviation
Full sample (9,840 observations)					
Logarithm of per capita daily expenditures	1.36	7.25	3.86	3.83	0.62
Agricultural development district is Karonga	0	1	0.05	0	0.21
Agricultural development district is Mzuzu	0	1	0.10	0	0.30
Agricultural development district is Kasungu	0	1	0.12	0	0.33
Agricultural development district is Salima	0	1	0.05	0	0.23
Agricultural development district is Lilongwe	0	1	0.21	0	0.41
Agricultural development district is Machinga	0	1	0.20	0	0.40
Agricultural development district is Blantyre	0	1	0.20	0	0.40
Agricultural development district is Ngabu	0	1	0.07	0	0.26
Household size	1	27	4.57	4	2.34
Number of members who can read in English	0	9	0.87	0	1.2
Highest educational qualification acquired in household is Junior Certificate of Education (JCE)	0	1	0.10	0	0.31
Household head can read in Chichewa	0	1	0.62	1	0.48
Number of male adults in the household	0	8	1.08	1	0.82
Household grew tobacco in past five cropping seasons	0	1	0.20	0	0.40
Floor of main dwelling is predominantly made of smooth cement	0	1	0.14	0	0.34
Number of separate rooms occupied by household, excluding toilet, storeroom, or garage	0	16	2.50	2	1.30
Any household member sleeps under a bed net?	0	1	0.37	0	0.48
Cooking fuel is collected firewood	0	1	0.84	1	0.36
Bed ownership	0	1	0.27	0	0.44
Tape, CD player, or HiFi ownership	0	1	0.12	0	0.33
Electric, gas stove, or hot plate ownership	0	1	0.01	0	0.09
Bicycle ownership	0	1	0.38	0	0.49
Paraffin lantern ownership	0	1	0.64	1	0.48
Panga ownership	0	1	0.30	0	0.46
Wireless radio ownership	0	1	0.55	1	0.49
Lighting fuel is electricity	0	1	0.02	0	0.14
Rubbish disposal facility is public rubbish heap	0	1	0.19	0	0.39

Source: Own results based on Malawi IHS2 data. Panga is a large heavy knife used for cutting vegetation.

Appendix 4. Descriptive statistics of variables used in the rural model (calibration sample)

Variable label	Minimum	Maximum	Mean	Median	Standard Deviation
Calibration sample (6,560 observations)					
Logarithm of per capita daily expenditures	1.36	7.25	3.87	3.83	0.61
Agricultural development district is Karonga	0	1	0.05	0	0.22
Agricultural development district is Mzuzu	0	1	0.10	0	0.30
Agricultural development district is Kasungu	0	1	0.12	0	0.33
Agricultural development district is Salima	0	1	0.06	0	0.23
Agricultural development district is Lilongwe	0	1	0.21	0	0.41
Agricultural development district is Machinga	0	1	0.20	0	0.40
Agricultural development district is Blantyre	0	1	0.20	0	0.40
Agricultural development district is Ngabu	0	1	0.07	0	0.26
Household size	1	18	4.61	4	2.33
Number of members who can read in English	0	8	0.87	0	1.20
Highest educational qualification acquired in household is Junior Certificate of Education (JCE)	0	1	0.10	0	0.30
Household head can read in Chichewa	0	1	0.62	1	0.48
Number of male adults in the household	0	8	1.08	1	0.82
Household grew tobacco in past five cropping seasons	0	1	0.20	0	0.40
Floor of main dwelling is predominantly made	0	1	0.14	0	0.34
Number of separate rooms occupied by household, excluding toilet, storeroom, or garage	0	16	2.52	2	1.32
Any household member sleeps under a bed net?	0	1	0.37	0	0.48
Cooking fuel is collected firewood	0	1	0.84	1	0.36
Bed ownership	0	1	0.27	0	0.44
Tape, CD player, or HiFi ownership	0	1	0.12	0	0.33
Electric, gas stove, or hot plate ownership	0	1	0.01	0	0.09
Bicycle ownership	0	1	0.38	0	0.49
Paraffin lantern ownership	0	1	0.65	1	0.48
Panga ownership	0	1	0.30	0	0.46
Wireless radio ownership	0	1	0.54	1	0.50
Lighting fuel is electricity	0	1	0.02	0	0.14
Rubbish disposal facility is public rubbish heap	0	1	0.18	0	0.39

Source: Own results based on Malawi IHS2 data. Panga is a large heavy knife used for cutting vegetation.

Appendix 5. Descriptive statistics of variables used in the rural model (validation sample)

Variable label	Minimum	Maximum	Mean	Median	Standard Deviation
Validation sample (3,280 observations)					
Logarithm of per capita daily expenditures	2.00	6.76	3.87	3.83	0.63
Agricultural development district is Karonga	0	1	0.05	0	0.22
Agricultural development district is Mzuzu	0	1	0.10	0	0.30
Agricultural development district is Kasungu	0	1	0.12	0	0.33
Agricultural development district is Salima	0	1	0.05	0	0.22
Agricultural development district is Lilongwe	0	1	0.22	0	0.41
Agricultural development district is Machinga	0	1	0.20	0	0.40
Agricultural development district is Blantyre	0	1	0.20	0	0.40
Agricultural development district is Ngabu	0	1	0.07	0	0.26
Household size	1	27	4.50	4	2.34
Number of members who can read in English	0	9	0.86	0	1.19
Highest educational qualification acquired in household is Junior Certificate of Education (JCE)	0	1	1.1	0	0.31
Household head can read in Chichewa	0	1	0.62	1	0.49
Number of male adults in the household	0	6	1.07	1	0.81
Household grew tobacco in past five cropping seasons	0	1	0.20	0	0.40
Floor of main dwelling is predominantly made of smooth cement	0	1	0.13	0	0.34
Number of separate rooms occupied by household, excluding toilet, storeroom, or garage	0	13	2.46	2	1.27
Any household member sleeps under a bed net?	0	1	0.37	0	0.48
Cooking fuel is collected firewood	0	1	0.83	1	0.37
Bed ownership	0	1	0.27	0	0.44
Tape, CD player, or HiFi ownership	0	1	0.13	0	0.33
Electric, gas stove, or hot plate ownership	0	1	0.01	0	0.09
Bicycle ownership	0	1	0.39	0	0.49
Paraffin lantern ownership	0	1	0.63	1	0.48
Panga ownership	0	1	0.31	0	0.46
Wireless radio ownership	0	1	0.57	1	0.50
Lighting fuel is electricity	0	1	0.02	0	0.14
Rubbish disposal facility is public rubbish heap	0	1	0.19	0	0.39

Source: Own results based on Malawi IHS2 data. Panga is a large heavy knife used for cutting vegetation.

Appendix 6. Descriptive statistics of variables used in the urban model (full sample)

Variable label	Minimum	Maximum	Mean	Median	Standard Deviation
Full sample (1,440 observations)					
Logarithm of per capita daily expenditures	2.53	7.65	4.45	4.36	0.81
Mzuzu city	0	1	0.17	0	0.37
Lilongwe city	0	1	0.33	0	0.47
Zomba city	0	1	0.17	0	0.37
Blantyre city	0	1	0.33	0	0.47
Household size	1	15	4.36	4	2.32
Number of members who can read in English	0	12	1.83	1	1.81
Household head can read in Chichewa	0	1	0.85	1	0.36
Highest class level ever attended by females in the household is secondary/post primary	0	1	0.31	0	0.46
Highest class level ever attended by members is superior or post-secondary	0	1	0.08	0	0.28
Household has a cellular phone in working condition	0	1	0.17	0	0.38
Household owns a landline telephone in working condition	0	1	0.05	0	0.22
Cooking fuel is collected firewood	0	1	0.15	0	0.35
Lighting fuel is electricity	0	1	0.32	0	0.47
Bed ownership	0	1	0.67	1	0.47
Television & VCR ownership	0	1	0.18	0	0.39
Electric, gas stove, or hot plate ownership	0	1	0.15	0	0.35
Sewing machine ownership	0	1	0.04	0	0.20
Number of separate rooms occupied by household, excluding toilet, storeroom, or garage	0	10	2.53	2	1.28
Dwelling construction material is traditional	0	1	0.21	0	0.41
Household head sleeps on Mat (grass) on floor	0	1	0.27	0	0.44
Household has no toilet facility	0	1	0.03	0	0.17
Floor of main dwelling is predominantly made of smoothed cement	0	1	0.63	1	0.48
Is there a place to purchase common medicines, such as panadol in this community?	0	1	0.93	1	0.25

Source: Own results based on Malawi IHS2 data.

Appendix 7. Descriptive statistics of variables used in the urban model (calibration sample)

Variable label	Minimum	Maximum	Mean	Median	Standard Deviation
Calibration sample (960 observations)					
Logarithm of per capita daily expenditures	2.53	7.50	4.48	4.37	0.83
Mzuzu city	0	1	0.17	0	0.37
Lilongwe city	0	1	0.33	0	0.47
Zomba city	0	1	0.17	0	0.37
Blantyre city	0	1	0.33	0	0.47
Household size	1	15	4.24	4	2.26
Number of members who can read in English	0	10	1.72	1	1.69
Household head can read in Chichewa	0	1	0.84	1	0.36
Highest class level ever attended by females in the household is secondary/post primary	0	1	0.30	0	0.46
Highest class level ever attended by members is superior or post-secondary	0	1	0.09	0	0.28
Household has a cellular phone in working condition	0	1	0.17	0	0.37
Household owns a landline telephone in working condition	0	1	0.05	0	0.22
Cooking fuel is collected firewood	0	1	0.14	0	0.35
Lighting fuel is electricity	0	1	0.31	0	0.46
Bed ownership	0	1	0.67	1	0.47
Television & VCR ownership	0	1	0.16	0	0.37
Electric, gas stove, or hot plate ownership	0	1	0.14	0	0.34
Sewing machine ownership	0	1	0.05	0	0.21
Number of separate rooms occupied by household, excluding toilet, storeroom, or garage	1	10	2.53	2	1.31
Dwelling construction material is traditional	0	1	0.22	0	0.41
Household head sleeps on Mat (grass) on floor	0	1	0.27	0	0.44
Household has no toilet facility	0	1	0.02	0	0.15
Floor of main dwelling is predominantly made of smoothed cement	0	1	0.63	1	0.48
Is there a place to purchase common medicines, such as panadol in this community?	0	1	0.93	1	0.25

Source: Own results based on Malawi IHS2 data.

Appendix 8. Descriptive statistics of variables used in the urban model (validation sample)

Variable label	Mini-	Maxi-	Mean	Median	Standard
Validation sample (480 observations)					
Logarithm of per capita daily expenditures	2.64	7.65	4.40	4.35	0.77
Mzuzu city	0	1	0.17	0	0.37
Lilongwe city	0	1	0.33	0	0.47
Zomba city	0	1	0.17	0	0.37
Blantyre city	0	1	0.33	0	0.47
Household size	1	14	4.62	4	2.41
Number of members who can read in English	0	1	2.04	2	2.01
Household head can read in Chichewa	0	1	0.86	1	0.35
Highest class level ever attended by females in the household is secondary/post primary	0	1	0.32	0	0.47
Highest class level ever attended by members is superior or post-secondary	0	1	0.08	0	0.27
Household has a cellular phone in working condition	0	1	0.19	0	0.39
Household owns a landline telephone in working condition	0	1	0.05	0	0.21
Cooking fuel is collected firewood	0	1	0.15	0	0.36
Lighting fuel is electricity	0	1	0.35	0	0.48
Bed ownership	0	1	0.67	1	0.47
Television & VCR ownership	0	1	0.22	0	0.41
Electric, gas stove, or hot plate ownership	0	1	0.16	0	0.37
Sewing machine ownership	0	1	0.04	0	0.19
Number of separate rooms occupied by household, excluding toilet, storeroom, or garage	0	8	2.52	2	1.23
Dwelling construction material is traditional	0	1	0.20	0	0.40
Household head sleeps on Mat (grass) on floor	0	1	0.28	0	0.45
Household has no toilet facility	0	1	0.04	0	0.20
Floor of main dwelling is predominantly made of smoothed cement	0	1	0.62	1	0.49
Is there a place to purchase common medicines, such as panadol in this community?	0	1	0.93	1	0.26

Source: Own results based on Malawi IHS2 data.

Development Economics and Policy

Series edited by Franz Heidhues, Joachim von Braun and Manfred Zeller

Band 1 Andrea Fadani: Agricultural Price Policy and Export and Food Production in Cameroon. A Farming Systems Analysis of Pricing Policies. The Case of Coffee-Based Farming Systems. 1999.

Band 2 Heike Michelsen: Auswirkungen der Währungsunion auf den Strukturanpassungsprozeß der Länder der afrikanischen Franc-Zone. 1995.

Band 3 Stephan Bea: Direktinvestitionen in Entwicklungsländern. Auswirkungen von Stabilisierungsmaßnahmen und Strukturreformen in Mexiko. 1995.

Band 4 Franz Heidhues / François Kamajou: Agricultural Policy Analysis – Proceedings of an International Seminar, held at the University of Dschang, Cameroon on May 26 and 27 1994, funded by the European Union under the Science and Technology Program (STD). 1996.

Band 5 Elke M. Förster: Protection or Liberalization? A Policy Analysis of the Korean Beef Sector. 1996.

Band 6 Gertrud Schrieder: The Role of Rural Finance for Food Security of the Poor in Cameroon. 1996.

Band 7 Nestor R. Ahoyo Adjovi: Economie des Systèmes de Production intégrant la Culture de Riz au Sud du Bénin: Potentialités, Contraintes et Perspectives. 1996.

Band 8 Jenny Müller: Income Distribution in the Agricultural Sector of Thailand. Empirical Analysis and Policy Options. 1996.

Band 9 Michael Brüntrup: Agricultural Price Policy and its Impact on Production, Income, Employment and the Adoption of Innovations. A Farming Systems Based Analysis of Cotton Policy in Northern Benin. 1997.

Band 10 Justin Bomda: Déterminants de l'Epargne et du Crédit, et leurs Implications pour le Développement du Système Financier Rural au Cameroun. 1998.

Band 11 John M. Msuya: Nutrition Improvement Projects in Tanzania: Implementation, Determinants of Performance, and Policy Implications. 1998.

Band 12 Andreas Neef: Auswirkungen von Bodenrechtswandel auf Ressourcennutzung und wirtschaftliches Verhalten von Kleinbauern in Niger und Benin. 1999.

Band 13 Susanna Wolf (ed.): The Future of EU-ACP Relations. 1999.

Band 14 Franz Heidhues / Gertrud Schrieder (eds.): Romania – Rural Finance in Transition Economies. 2000.

Band 15 Katinka Weinberger: Women's Participation. An Economic Analysis in Rural Chad and Pakistan. 2000.

Band 16 Christof Batzlen: Migration and Economic Development. Remittances and Investments in South Asia: A Case Study of Pakistan. 2000.

Band 17 Matin Qaim: Potential Impacts of Crop Biotechnology in Developing Countries. 2000.

Band 18 Jean Senahoun: Programmes d'ajustement structurel, sécurité alimentaire et durabilité agricole. Une approche d'analyse intégrée, appliquée au Bénin. 2001.

Band 19 Torsten Feldbrügge: Economics of Emergency Relief Management in Developing Countries. With Case Studies on Food Relief in Angola and Mozambique. 2001.

Band 20 Claudia Ringler: Optimal Allocation and Use of Water Resources in the Mekong River Basin: Multi-Country and Intersectoral Analyses. 2001.

Band 21 Arnim Kuhn: Handelskosten und regionale (Des-)Integration. Russlands Agrarmärkte in der Transformation. 2001.

Band 22 Ortrun Anne Gronski: Stock Markets and Economic Growth. Evidence from South Africa. 2001.

Band 23 Patrick Webb / Katinka Weinberger (eds.): Women Farmers. Enhancing Rights, Recognition and Productivity. 2001.

Band 24 Mingzhi Sheng: Lebensmittelkonsum und -konsumtrends in China. Eine empirische Analyse auf der Basis ökonometrischer Nachfragemodelle. 2002.

Band 25 Maria Iskandarani: Economics of Household Water Security in Jordan. 2002.

Band 26 Romeo Bertolini: Telecommunication Services in Sub-Saharan Africa. An Analysis of Access and Use in the Southern Volta Region in Ghana. 2002.

Band 27 Dietrich Müller-Falcke: Use and Impact of Information and Communication Technologies in Developing Countries' Small Businesses. Evidence from Indian Small Scale Industry. 2002.

Band 28 Wolfram Erhardt: Financial Markets for Small Enterprises in Urban and Rural Northern Thailand. Empirical Analysis on the Demand for and Supply of Financial Services, with Particular Emphasis on the Determinants of Credit Access and Borrower Transaction Costs. 2002.

Band 29 Wensheng Wang: The Impact of Information and Communication Technologies on Farm Households in China. 2002.

Band 30 Shyamal K. Chowdhury: Institutional and Welfare Aspects of the Provision and Use of Information and Communication Technologies in the Rural Areas of Bangladesh and Peru. 2002.

Band 31 Annette Luibrand: Transition in Vietnam. Impact of the Rural Reform Process on an Ethnic Minority. 2002.

Band 32 Felix Ankomah Asante: Economic Analysis of Decentralisation in Rural Ghana. 2003.

Band 33 Chodechai Suwanaporn: Determinants of Bank Lending in Thailand: An Empirical Examination for the Years 1992 to 1996. 2003.

Band 34 Abay Asfaw: Costs of Illness, Demand for Medical Care, and the Prospect of Community Health Insurance Schemes in the Rural Areas of Ethiopia. 2003.

Band 35 Gi-Soon Song: The Impact of Information and Communication Technologies (ICTs) on Rural Households. A Holistic Approach Applied to the Case of Lao People's Democratic Re- public. 2003.

Band 36 Daniela Lohlein: An Economic Analysis of Public Good Provision in Rural Russia. The Case of Education and Health Care. 2003.

Band 37 Johannes Woelcke. Bio-Economics of Sustainable Land Management in Uganda. 2003.

Band 38 Susanne M. Ziemek: The Economics of Volunteer Labor Supply. An Application to Countries of a Different Development Level. 2003.

Band 39 Doris Wiesmann: An International Nutrition Index. Concept and Analyses of Food Insecurity and Undernutrition at Country Levels. 2004.

Band 40 Isaac Osei-Akoto: The Economics of Rural Health Insurance. The Effects of Formal and Informal Risk-Sharing Schemes in Ghana. 2004.

Band 41 Yuansheng Jiang: Health Insurance Demand and Health Risk Management in Rural China. 2004.

Band 42 Roukayatou Zimmermann: Biotechnology and Value-added Traits in Food Crops: Relevance for Developing Countries and Economic Analyses. 2004.

Band 43 F. Markus Kaiser: Incentives in Community-based Health Insurance Schemes. 2004.

Band 44 Thomas Herzfeld: *Corruption begets Corruption*. Zur Dynamik und Persistenz der Korruption. 2004.

Band 45 Edilegnaw Wale Zegeye: The Economics of On-Farm Conservation of Crop Diversity in Ethiopia: Incentives, Attribute Preferences and Opportunity Costs of Maintaining Local Varieties of Crops. 2004.

Band 46 Adama Konseiga: Regional Integration Beyond the Traditional Trade Benefits: Labor Mobility contribution. The Case of Burkina Faso and Côte d'Ivoire. 2005.

Band 47 Beyene Tadesse Ferenji: The Impact of Policy Reform and Institutional Transformation on Agricultural Performance. An Economic Study of Ethiopian Agriculture. 2005.

Band 48 Sabine Daude: Agricultural Trade Liberalization in the WTO and Its Poverty Implications. A Study of Rural Households in Northern Vietnam. 2005.

Band 49 Kadir Osman Gyasi: Determinants of Success of Collective Action on Local Commons. An Empirical Analysis of Community-Based Irrigation Management in Northern Ghana. 2005.

Band 50 Borbala E. Balint: Determinants of Commercial Orientation and Sustainability of Agricultural Production of the Individual Farms in Romania. 2006.

Band 51 Pamela Marinda: Effects of Gender Inequality in Resource Ownership and Access on Household Welfare and Food Security in Kenya. A Case Study of West Pokot District. 2006.

Band 52 Charles Palmer: The Outcomes and their Determinants from Community-Company Contracting over Forest Use in Post-Decentralization Indonesia. 2006.

Band 53 Hardwick Tchale: Agricultural Policy and Soil Fertility Management in the Maize-based Smallholder Farming System in Malawi. 2006.

Band 54 John Kedi Mduma: Rural Off-Farm Employment and its Effects on Adoption of Labor Intensive Soil Conserving Measures in Tanzania. 2006.

Band 55 Mareike Meyn: The Impact of EU Free Trade Agreements on Economic Development and Regional Integration in Southern Africa. The Example of EU-SACU Trade Relations. 2006.

Band 56 Clemens Breisinger: Modelling Infrastructure Investments, Growth and Poverty Impact. A Two-Region Computable General Equilibrium Perspective on Vietnam. 2006.

Band 57 Meike Wollni: Coping with the Coffee Crisis. An Analysis of the Production and Marketing Performance of Coffee Farmers in Costa Rica. 2007.

Band 58 Franklin Simtowe: Performance and Impact of Microfinance. Evidence from Joint Liability Lending Programs in Malawi. 2008.

Band 59 Xiangping Jia: Credit Rationing and Institutional Constraint. Evidence from Rural China. 2008.

Band 60 Holger Seebens: The Economics of Gender and the Household in Developing Countries. 2009.

Band 61 Stephan Piotrowski: Land Property Rights and Natural Resource Use. An Analysis of Household Behavior in Rural China. 2009.

Band 62 Sebastian M. Scholz: Rural Development through Carbon Finance. Forestry Projects under the Clean Development Mechanism of the Kyoto Protocol. Assessing Smallholder Participation by Structural Equation Modeling. 2009.

Band 63 Jakob Rupert Friederichsen: Opening Up Knowledge Production through Participatory Research? Agricultural Research for Vietnam's Northern Uplands. 2009.

Band 64 Olivier Ecker: Economics of Micronutrient Malnutrition. The Demand for Nutrients in Sub-Saharan Africa. 2009.

Band 65 Julia Johannsen: Operational Assessment of Monetary Poverty by Proxy Means Tests. 2009

Band 66 Ephraim Nkonya / Nicolas Gerber / Philipp Baumgartner / Joachim von Braun / Alessandro De Pinto / Valerie Graw / Edward Kato / Julia Kloos / Teresa Walter: The Economics of Land Degradation. Toward an Integrated Global Assessment. 2011.

Band 67 S. Idriss Nazaire Houssou: Operational Poverty Targeting by Proxy Means Tests. Models and Policy Simulations for Malawi. 2013.

www.peterlang.de

FSC
www.fsc.org
MIX
Papier | Fördert gute Waldnutzung
FSC® C083411

Kolibri 360 GmbH
Ferdinand-Jühlke-Straße 7
99095 Erfurt, Deutschland
produktsicherheit@kolibri360.de